This book will grab you from the very first page, how an unlikely romance grew into a flourishing life-partnership and search for answers. An unconventional but truly beautiful love story, which I witnessed at close quarters for over forty-two years.

You will share their extraordinary journey together, their views on life, education, religion and the law (they both won university degrees in law, she at the age of seventy-six). How she helped him from 'lost child' to self-sufficient adult, how children and adults were drawn to her, how to nurture and educate children, and in doing what is 'right'. A tribute to a wonderful woman, her philosophy on life, and a personal quest that will challenge your beliefs.

The author, a former assistant golf professional, shows an intellect that far outstrips the needs of sport, proving him a serious student of the meaning of life. A thoroughly engaging read!

Brian Sparks, Performance Coach
and author of *Positive Impact Golf*

A ROSE
ON THE
DUNGHILL

The Reflections of a Fool on the Hill

JOHN AYRESS

Copyright © 2021 John Ayress

The moral right of the author has been asserted.

Apart from any fair dealing for the purposes of research or private study, or criticism or review, as permitted under the Copyright, Designs and Patents Act 1988, this publication may only be reproduced, stored or transmitted, in any form or by any means, with the prior permission in writing of the publishers, or in the case of reprographic reproduction in accordance with the terms of licences issued by the Copyright Licensing Agency. Enquiries concerning reproduction outside those terms should be sent to the publishers.

Matador
9 Priory Business Park,
Wistow Road, Kibworth Beauchamp,
Leicestershire. LE8 0RX
Tel: 0116 279 2299
Email: books@troubador.co.uk
Web: www.troubador.co.uk/matador
Twitter: @matadorbooks

ISBN 978 1 8004 6492 6

British Library Cataloguing in Publication Data.
A catalogue record for this book is available from the British Library.

Printed and bound in Great Britain by 4edge Limited
Typeset in 11pt Sabon by Troubador Publishing Ltd, Leicester, UK

Matador is an imprint of Troubador Publishing Ltd

In loving memory of Tony, my soul mate and fellow seeker.

Contents

Note to the Reader   ix

1	A Firm Footing	1
2	Breaking the Chain	10
3	Birds of Paradise	21
4	Lost in Paradise	34
5	A Rose, a Sweet, Sweet Rose	53
6	Forward to the Past	66
7	The Long Way Home	81
8	Amor Fati	100

Bibliography   112
Acknowledgements   114

Note to the Reader

In the summer of 1976 I was twenty, an assistant golf-pro, unhappy and lacking any real purpose in life, when a miracle happened – I met Antonia! Tony, as she preferred to be called, was Dutch, on holiday with her husband in England, and came to our golf club for lessons. She entered our shop wearing a dark blue, low-cut polo shirt and light blue trousers, a perfect picture! Despite the age difference (she was thirty years older), I was swept off my feet; it was love at first sight. As we walked off to the driving range, I couldn't take my eyes off her and remember blurting out the words, "Why can't people love each other?" (what an opening line!), and from that moment, we were hooked. Little did we know that this would lead to a relationship that was to last for forty wonderful years, until she finally gave way to Alzheimer's in October 2018.

Tony was a joy and inspiration not only to me but to all who had the privilege of knowing her. She was the metaphorical rose on the dunghill, a radiant, beacon of hope. If there *are* angels on earth, she was one of them. Which leaves me, the fool on the hill, to write a book in her honour and to pass on her love, wisdom and example. This, I feel, is the least I can do.

Though this book is dedicated to her, it is not a biography of her life. As the metaphors in the title suggest, it recounts our adventure together and our search for answers. The result is a conscious blend of the biographical and autobiographical; not a chronological review of dates, places, persons and events but a selection of ideas and episodes that illustrate *our* reflections on the meaning of life. In particular, our struggle with faith and the nature of man on the one hand and the concepts of culture, tradition and society on the other. At times, they assume a distinct religious flavour, while at others take on a more philosophical or socio-psychological strain.

As the narrative unfolds, I recall personal stories meaningful to us *and* look at the experiences and writings of others. These, Dear Reader, I wish to share with you, in the hope that they may help you in your attempt to understand the world we live in. I don't know who will read them – not important – what matters is the sharing. They may go on to germinate and lead a life of their own, or wither and perish 'as wind in dry grass'. Should just *one* reader find consolation or interest in these words, then my undertaking was not in vain. That, at least, is a comforting thought!

Finally, I should add that this fool on the hill has no other weapons other than the tiresome introspection of the dreamer, together with a modest talent for poetry, prose, drawing and musical composition. Nevertheless, I promise you a good read!

*'And he shall be like a tree
planted by the rivers of water.'*

The Bible, Psalm I:3

Chapter One
A Firm Footing

I am sure we all struggle with the meaning of life; I certainly do. During childhood, I had countless questions but few answers. I remember the huge excitement when I 'discovered' history; wow, such amazing stories, surely the answers will be found there? Every week, I would add another title to my growing collection of *Ladybird Histories* books: Cleopatra, Julius Caesar, Napoleon, no end of names, but with every book, the questions only grew! And there was history at school too; all I had to do was ask, but the history master was a huge, intimidating man whom we all dreaded. He would have us in single files before the classroom door, boys to the left, girls to the right, and upon entering, we were ordered to sit down quickly… and I mean quickly. For we were barely seated when he would start hurling our textbooks through the air like missiles. Those seated at the back would have to get up again to retrieve their books, which had fallen dismally short of the mark, while those in the front would be lucky not to be struck in the face by a direct hit! So, you can imagine my trepidation when, on that fateful day after his lesson on the Norman Conquest, like Oliver Twist asking for *more*,[1] I dared to ask him if that was *all*.

"*All*," he roared. "There's enough work there for the whole semester... be off with you boy!"

My enthusiasm for history died on that day. It took me ten years to recover my pride before picking up a history book again. (Cries of lament!)

Life sucks, we are told – deal with it! This is easier said than done. Tony insisted that just as plants need sunlight and water, so do we need love and attention, especially during the *first three years* of our lives. Happy mum, happy baby. It gives us a firm footing... how else can we cope with what life throws at us?

Hmm, and have I coped? I mean, come on, it took me ten years to get over that history setback and I'm still harping on about it fifty years later – at least it was significant enough to get this book started! If the first three years *are* essential for a firm footing, then presumably the better the upbringing (software), the greater the ability to thrive, irrespective of one's genetic code (hardware). I suppose the evolutionists would argue that nurture doesn't come into it; you either make it or you don't ('survival of the fittest'). 'If a plant cannot live according to its nature', says Thoreau, 'it dies; and so man'.[2] I guess both views have a point.

Anyway, to return to the autobiographical facts of my life. Born in 1956 (into the literary 'Angry Young Men' generation, for what it's worth) in post-war England, at Clacton-on-Sea of all places (that's in Essex, by the way, before you check your Google Maps), to middle-class parents – which involved, in our case, a grand tour of Southern England, from Clacton to Windsor to Bristol to Ware (where? Yes, that's right) and finally to Teignmouth (Devon) – where my parents' cross-country run of chasing work eventually came to a retiring halt. And during

---

1   Character and title of a novel by Charles Dickens (1838), who asks for more broth in the orphan house.
2   Henry David Thoreau, *Civil Disobedience*, 285.

all of this, I enjoyed a traditional English upbringing of 'no sex please, we're British', and that in the sixties!

One significant consequence of all this flitting about, was that I somehow missed the 'eleven-plus exam', which was not then uniform throughout the whole country. This was a compulsory test for eleven-year-olds to determine the next step: grammar school or secondary. The teachers recommended secondary, and my parents took their 'advice' with exemplary good faith (the teacher knows best). If they had been a little more assertive, I could have ended up going to grammar school and been spared that fateful history incident. The notion of 'civil disobedience' obviously hadn't yet grabbed them. Ah, how precarious is the lifeline we present our children with. A firm footing indeed!

Another consequence was that it sparked a desire to travel. Though having never ventured further north than Luton or further south than the holiday destinations of the Isle of Wight and Guernsey, I did persuade my parents to let me visit Europe on two occasions: a school trip to Ostend in Belgium and then another to Paris in France. I distinctly remember the exhilaration of leaving behind the familiar coastline of Kent and the prospect of setting foot on new shores abroad. My world view was definitely expanding!

Born in 1956, is that significant, too? Musically perhaps, for Mozart was born in 1756 and J.S. Bach even shares my birthday: 21st March. Well, I could have done worse! And what about Clacton-on-Sea? Well, it's situated next to Klein Holland, a modest estate owned by the Dutch royal family (it was their sanctuary during World War II) and usually referred to as Holland-on-Sea. It's tempting to see this as a forebode – Tony was Dutch, and I was to spend the greater part of my life living and working in Holland.

These then, would appear to be the principal ingredients to the question: who am I? An Englishman with a shared musical heritage (!), an urge to travel (with a bias for Holland, Belgium and France), a fear of flying, snakes and dogs but not cows (sorry, forgot to mention those) and an education with disappointing results. Now, before we move on, let me first tell you about the snakes, dogs and cows (perhaps not the choicest of subjects, but there we are).

As the naturalist of the family, my brother had many wildlife books full of large and vivid pictures. Turning the pages, especially those with snakes of all shapes and sizes, sent shivers down my spine, which did not go unnoticed. Thus, my dear, sadistic brother, would place a book opposite my bedroom door, opened at a page showing a particularly menacing snake, and, to rub it in, *also* put one of those very life-like rubber snakes in my bed! Well, he couldn't help it really; I mean, what would you do? Remind me to pay him back one day for his kindness! And Dad, where were you in all this?

The sage and mystic G.I. Gurdjieff had the better mentor in this matter, for his father – we are told – 'would sometimes slip a frog, a worm, a mouse [...] into my bed, and would make me take non-poisonous snakes in my hands and even play with them', all with the purpose of engendering an 'attitude of indifference' to impulses such as 'fastidiousness, repulsion, squeamishness, fear, timidity and so on'. 'If it had not been for this', he concludes, 'I would never have been able to overcome all the obstacles and difficulties that I had to encounter later during my travels'.[3]

If his father had a powerful influence, so too did Gurdjieff's first tutor, Dean Borsch. He insisted that from early childhood there should be instilled in the child:

'Belief in receiving punishment for disobedience. Hope of receiving reward only for merit. Love of God – but indifference to the saints. Remorse of conscience for the ill-treatment of animals. Fear of grieving parents and teachers. Fearlessness

---

3   *Meetings with Remarkable Men*, 44–45, a fascinating read.

towards devils, snakes and mice. Joy in being content with what one has. Sorrow at the loss of the goodwill of others. Patient endurance of pain and hunger. The striving early to earn one's bread.'[4]

The reader will forgive the full quote (snakes and all), but this wisdom was too good to pass by.

If I was afraid of snakes, I was also afraid of dogs. It all started the day my parents introduced a dog into the family (we had a cat, but a dog too?). It was a small dog, probably only a puppy, but I was terrified of it. It would scratch frantically every morning from behind the kitchen door whenever it heard someone approach (usually me). I didn't know then that it was from joy at the expected company and the prospect of breakfast, so I just froze at the door, not daring to open it. In the end it was either me or the dog who would have to go – they got rid of the dog!

Then there was that large, nasty black dog on the way to school. It was always there, waiting for me. It knew I had to pass; the alternative involved a huge detour which I tried once, only to find him there too, grinning with defiant malice! He had won; I was defeated... or was I? It was now either him or me. I don't remember where I got the courage from, but I do remember (and shall never forget) the expression on its face when I walked straight past him like he didn't exist! He didn't growl or follow me, just dropped his jaw in astonishment. My fear of dogs disappeared on that day.

I now appreciate the wonderful advice in the refrain of the Val Doonican song, 'Walk Tall'.[5]

Now, with the cows the roles were reversed – I wasn't afraid of them, but my mother was! It must have been one of my earliest memories, seeing some cows grazing in our front garden (which

---

4   ibid, 57.
5   'Walk Tall', song by Val Doonican (1964) with its brilliant refrain!

was a feat in itself because it was only a small plot). Legend has it, that I went out to confront them with a stick and tried to persuade them to return to the field opposite where they had come from. What I remember most is their eyes (cows have lovely eyes and, I'm told, can even jump over the moon!) and also those of my mother, terror-stricken, as she watched my antics from the safety of our living room. I felt quite a hero, akin to the first awakenings of the Oedipus complex.[6]

If I did hold any amorous feelings towards my mother, they were soon swept away on the turbulent seas of her nervous energy. There was always an element of unrest lurking about her, a tension that could easily erupt into an awkward scene. Hardly favourable towards intimacy! If she didn't get her way, neither did we, including my father. It was her who told us what to do and how to do it, what to eat and how to eat it. A classic control freak, but one whose outward bravura masked an inner insecurity. I only gained this insight later, after learning that she was an adopted child; until then however, I was suffocating rather than wallowing in her affection. I should add here Tony's view that there are two types of mothers: those who dote on the children and those who bestow their affection on the father. My mother categorically belonged to the latter. She was lost without him.

So, if I didn't end up marrying my mother (that was reserved for Tony!), did I wish to kill my father? No, that would be unfair for I didn't hate him. Yes, we did argue and fall out sometimes. Yes, I often cowered before his standard of perfection but, on balance, my feeling towards him was benign. This needs some clarification.

My father was often sarcastic in his views, yet honest, practical and persistent in his endeavours. He was also a perfectionist; he didn't trust others to do anything right, myself included. There lies the key to our relationship. What could I

---

[6] A concept in psychoanalysis derived from Greek mythology (Oedipus murders his father to marry his mother).

do to win his approval? I once made a small footstool at school (woodwork class) but on the way home decided to get rid of it and chucked it onto a nearby coal truck when nobody was looking. I presume the coalmen scratched their heads in bewilderment and put it down to 'pennies from heaven'! My mother still recalls this incident as I probably told her and not my father. Of course, he was good with his hands: mending things in the house, making wooden castles and farms for us to play with or constructing a garden shed. No task was too small, and he did it all without our help. We would only get in the way he said – collateral damage!

Ironically, his perfectionism was also the cause of his greatest frustration in life. As a young man he showed great promise as a pianist and studied towards a musical career. But during his final exam at the London School of Music, an inner voice spoke, "You're not Chopin, so why bother?" Devastating advice! So, he didn't. He gave it all up and became a civil servant, carrying a life-long grudge on his shoulder. He would still play at home, at somebody's request, but it always ended with him slamming down the piano lid and leaving the room in a huff. Only after retirement, when he no longer needed to prove himself, was he able to play again in a more relaxed manner.

Unfortunately, I never benefited from that. Instead, I had to grind through endless hours of joyless practice – scales, arpeggios etc – until it ended in tears. So, my parents opted for piano teachers, but they didn't help either. The first one had the crazy notion, because I was left-handed, of practising with the right hand only, to compensate as it were! Ridiculous! She was an old bat, anyway, and I didn't like her. The second one was nicer but lived much further away. It meant a good twenty-five minutes by bike and it was usually dark by the time I got there. I also had to pass by a graveyard, which didn't exactly help my enthusiasm! In short, like my father, I gave it up. Thanks for the example, Dad!

In his defence, he was a good dad. He was generally good-humoured and often played with us and took us out for walks in the countryside. We had fun playing in the park, collecting 'conkers' and sailing our boats on the lake. At sixteen, when he realised that I wanted to break free, he was very magnanimous and said he just wanted me to be happy, and he gave me some practical advice too: "Don't get into debt," he said. "And don't start shaving your sideburns too early." I respect and love him for that and have always followed his advice!

I have no doubt that my parents meant well and had my best interests at heart, but their actions, at times, ran counter to their intentions. Another mystic, Thomas Traherne, once remarked, 'It is not our parents' loins so much as our parents' lives that enthralls and blinds us'.[7] Parents make an impact, for better or for worse.

If *my* firm footing is questionable, Tony's is not. As an only child, she had love and attention in abundance, though was not spoiled. Her parents were devout Catholics, and both came from large families. She was rarely alone (with so many cousins to play with!) and had a very happy childhood. She adored her parents, particularly her father. In her diaries – which she started as a young girl and carried on until she was no longer able, due to Alzheimer's – there are many references to him as being the 'dearest father in the whole world'.

Yet as much as he loved his daughter, he was against her going away to study. During the war she had immersed herself in archaeology, classical art and literature (further education was limited) and showed considerable talent. She was offered the chance of an apprenticeship at the British Museum, but her father disapproved. He preferred to see his daughter married and raise a family as all good catholic girls should. This devastated Tony. Many years later she told me that this was the only time in her life that she had cursed her father. Yet out of love and respect

---

7   Colin Wilson, *The Outsider*, 314 (cited in his postscript to the 2001 edition).

for him, she resigned herself to his wishes, married the Protestant man to whom she was then engaged and reared four children!

Only thirty years later, after seeing all her children study and meeting me and encouraging me to study too, did she follow up her own dream. She studied law, took her degree and was over the moon! Even her father would have been proud, especially if he knew that she had forgiven him.

One diary entry written at that time captures just how much studying meant to her: 'please know', she writes, 'that if I die tomorrow [she was then working part-time at a jewellers and afraid of being attacked], I am happy. I'm now studying at last, with two fine student friends; I have four wonderful children, a lovely apartment and John is sweet'.

This introduction to Tony and myself now ends where it started, with the conclusion that love and attention during the first three years is the *sine qua non* for a firm footing, to be followed up with guidance and support during childhood. The bottom line is that parents should stand *behind* their children, encouraging them forward and not *in front* as obstacles to be overcome. How many children can boast that? Parents take heed! But not only parents. As a footnote we might add that though, in Western society, this responsibility does fall primarily on the parents, it is not their burden alone. Teachers, peers and others too, can play a pivotal role.

> *'Children are remarkably resilient if they are surrounded by love. If not, it can scar them for life.'*
>
> Charles Handy, *The Hungry Spirit*

Chapter Two

Breaking the Chain

Tony was devoted to her children and in a sense, I was her fifth child. The love and attention she bestowed in abundance on them was now unconditionally bestowed on me. Unaccustomed as I was to such affection, I didn't know how to handle it at first. It turned my emotional world upside down. Having had so little 'sunlight and water' for so long, the sudden infusion almost drowned me. In fact, it caused such a jolt that I needed therapy for two years! This was, of course, a necessary adjustment, a system reboot! Yet how blessed am I, for this was the path to my 'recovery'.

Tony knew instinctively that love and attention during the *first three years* forms the foundation. Happy mum, happy baby. She herself had received plenty as a child. Now, she had the opportunity to test her theory again, only this time, the 'child' was a young man (I was twenty-two when we started living together!). So, would the treatment work? We agreed that in *pathological* cases, remedy was not possible; a broken plant can't be healed, but an ailing one can. And here we differed. Tony believed that such a plant could, in time, be 'fully' restored, i.e. able to hold itself up *after* the cure. But I held that the plant was scarred for life. It was, as it were, a 'bottomless pit', i.e. in constant need of 'topping up', the amount or frequency depending on the degree of the deficiency. The wound might be healed, but the scar would remain. This difference of opinion, by the way, is purely academic, for we both agreed on the major premise: that ailing plants *should* be healed.[8]

And did the treatment help? Of course, it did – I'm the living proof! But whether 'fully' restored or in need of 'topping up', who can tell? To date, the signs appear to support Tony's view. No relapse or instances of other infantile behaviour. I feel strong. Looking at others, I discriminate between those thriving or ailing and am now able to help the latter for I can empathise with their needs. It may be true to say that a thriving plant is more likely to show altruism than its ailing counterpart. Statistically, there are far more ailing plants than thriving ones, a fact sadly, or perhaps gladly, overlooked.[9] The healthier plants thus have a lot of work on their hands! Yet they do not complain, for as they receive, so do they give.

Entering university was the ultimate opportunity for Tony to realise her ideas on upbringing. The thought of having these accepted within the academic community was a great motivating factor. Not that she needed it; after thirty years of waiting she was rearing to go! Psychology was her forte and seemed the obvious choice, but as that involved a considerable portion of statistics (ugh!), she opted for law instead. As I had already begun studying law, we were able to 'compare' notes. That helped her find the suitable fields to focus on: criminal law, criminology and childcare.

At that time, during the nineties, the Netherlands witnessed a rise in the number of 'criminal' offences committed by offenders

---

8   The reader will forgive my comparing people to plants. It is a well-worn metaphor in literature.

9   In present-day healthcare the number of patients far exceeds the number of nurses.

under twelve years of age. Technically, this group was excluded from criminal law. The debate therefore centred on the question of whether to reduce the minimum age from twelve years to ten years. And if so, what measures exactly should be taken? A similar debate was also being held in England. There, changes to legislation were being prepared, allowing criminal courts more powers and measures. One such measure was the Parenting Order, that would 'offer parents training and help to change the offending behaviour of their children and may also direct parents to exercise more control'.[10] With this, courts could compel parents or guardians to attend training/guidance sessions. This was seen as the logical consequence of the parents' responsibility for the behaviour of their children.

This topic offered Tony the ideal platform and area of research. I remember vividly her excitement during this period as she visualised her dream becoming a legal reality! She was in full agreement with the developments in England and argued for their implementation in the Netherlands. She outlined and formulated the required changes to Dutch criminal law, stressing thereby the need for non-punitive measures. All this research she put into her thesis – the prevention of criminal offences committed by young offenders – and gave it the suggestive title, *Breaking the Chain*. The 'chain' was a symbol for a pattern of thought or ideas, i.e. parental commands. If this pattern led to 'criminal' behaviour, then the chain should be broken. If not, the dysfunctional behaviour would continue and may even be passed on from one generation to the next. Heaven forbid!

There is a sad irony in the fact that Tony finally completed her study in the new millennium (2000), after waiting most of her life in the old. Yes, it was her crowning achievement, but at seventy-six years of age it just came too late, at least from a career perspective. Within a small circle, her ideas did have an

---

10   Quoted from Tony's doctorate thesis, *Breaking the Chain* (Leiden, 2000), 39.

impact, but a wider recognition was not to be. She still had the energy and passion to proceed and many, including her children, admired her for it. She got involved in a number of projects that aimed to show that punishing young offenders was *not* the way forward. We were all amazed and alarmed when she took to visiting young offenders in prison 'just to talk with them', she said! Our bourgeois concern for her safety did not deter her, and rightly so, for who were we to stand in her way?

Then one day, she came home visibly shaken.

"What happened?" I asked.

She told me that she was well aware of the risks involved in visiting a prison. She had always relied on her sixth sense to warn her of any danger and nothing remotely threatening had ever happened. On the contrary, the boys she spoke with all opened up to her and some had even confided their dreams in life to her. Perhaps that had given her a false sense of security, or perhaps she had just been naive. Anyway, something happened that day that really frightened her. One of the boys had come up to her, was very agitated and said that she should leave at once. Why? Because some of the boys – the more hardened ones – were planning to break out.[11] From the workshop, they were going to pass through the nearest exit point, using her as leverage. She had indeed felt their restlessness and noticed some boys standing by the knives, looking nervous.

Luckily, one of the boys had intervened, saying, "No, not her, she's OK!"

Tony took the advice and left immediately.

After this incident, she never returned to another prison. Though she was terribly disappointed, her faith in her method was not shaken. All she wanted to do was 'make a difference' and actually help those who lacked love and attention. Young offenders fitted the bill. They were crying out for help, but the

---

11 The prison was a semi-open unit with several workshops and inmates had easy access to all sorts of tools, including knives and screwdrivers.

treatment they needed proved more than she could give. Yes, she could take on the whole world – who else would? Give them as much attention as possible, attention and still more attention, but best of all, she said, was *love*. And how can that be given to juvenile delinquents in a prison environment? The 'chain', Tony would reply, should have been broken *earlier*!

Not only did prison inmates open up to her, but children generally. She had something about her that made them smile, all of them! Whenever she entered a place – shop, cafe, church or school – the children there were immediately aware of her presence. Sometimes, they would just come up to her and tug on her sleeve, demanding attention, even though she was a complete stranger, and their parents had no say in the matter! And the reaction of babies, well, that was a wonder to behold. How often have I seen mothers just shake their heads in amazement? As Tony approached a baby lying in its pram or whatever, its eyes would widen and its face would turn into a huge, laughing grin. Sometimes, a baby would just raise its outstretched arms in gleeful expectation! And all this occurred naturally. Tony didn't need to do those silly adult things: pulling faces, stroking cheeks, playing with fingers or coo-cooing. It just happened!

Now, before the reader gets the wrong impression, there is another side to her personality that I must mention. Children adored her, that was obvious. But if they misbehaved, she would lose no time in correcting them. In a restaurant, for example, if there were some children running around and making a lot of noise, she would tell them to be quiet. "*Stil*," she would cry out (Dutch equivalent for quiet and her favourite word!) in a reprimanding tone so *they* got the message and it was also audible enough for the parents, to remind *them* of *their* lack of control. Which was the whole point.

Tony's own children were sometimes embarrassed at their mother's outspokenness, but they could also laugh about it because, in their hearts, they knew that she was only saying out loud what they were all thinking. Back in the restaurant, I never witnessed any parent come up to Tony and tell her to mind her own business. On the contrary, they actually made a real attempt to control their children! This is interesting because many people refrain from an outward show of social control, out of fear of incurring the parent's wrath. They resort instead to indirect hinting and body language and rarely dare to speak *directly* to the offending children. Tony explained this as follows:

Parents find it difficult to get the balance right. They are either too strict and uncompromising or the very opposite: too timid and lenient. In the former, there is tension and no fun, in the latter all play and no rules. Yet children need both play *and* rules. If the parents get the balance right, then a firm footing is guaranteed! But this success is chiefly dependent on chance and, unfortunately, few parents get it right. Most struggle with the upbringing of their children and rarely admit it. They are reluctant to seek help and thus receive no other training than the bias and subjective example of *their* parents. Social control from other adults will also likely oscillate between these two extremes. Children are thus told constantly, either what to do or, to do what they like. In addition, on the scale between these extremes, lies a whole range of potentially conflicting parental commands. 'Yes, you go out and play and leave your poor mother here!' The end result is a proliferation of either neurotic or narcissistic behaviour. This is what happens when the education of children is entrusted solely to parents who are insufficiently prepared for the task.

This style of upbringing is a defining characteristic of Western European culture. Primarily, it is *not* in the interest of the child but in the interest of the society to which the child belongs. I mention this here in passing and will return to this phenomenon in the final chapter.

As a young mother enjoying a beach holiday with her family, often in Spain, Tony invariably found herself surrounded by other people's children. Whether from tourists or locals, these kids would just gravitate towards her and join in the fun.

On one such occasion, a German tourist, seeing all these children and assuming they were Tony's, came up to her and said: "*Du bist eine Gute Mutter, mit viele Söhne.*" (you must be a good mother with so many sons)! Of course, he was just flirting, but that's beside the point, and she was used to that, anyway. If Tony was to pick up a flute and start playing, she would have hordes of children running after her just like the Pied Piper of Hamelin![12]

At home, what started as a family ritual soon became a local institution. Tony made it a rule to be *at home* when her children got back from school, ready with tea and cake. This was the highlight of the day. Her kids would tell all their stories and she would listen. Word soon spread and, before long, most of the neighbourhood kids also came along for tea and cake. But it wasn't just about the tea and cake. It was all about the love and attention that many of them missed at home. How many kids today can boast of a mother who *will be at home*, waiting for them with tea and cake? How many mothers today are caught between working at the office and raising kids at home? They will argue that it's a question of 'prioritising' or 'finding the right balance'. How convenient to forget the need for a firm footing? Yes, show me just one who says she can do it, and I will burst her bubble!

I can now hear you objecting that in idealising Tony, I have started to overstate the case. There may be some truth in that. In defence, I would answer, yes, but it's worth overstating! It is a case so simple, yet so important that it cannot be stressed enough. Back in 1950, Erik Erikson already noted the use of 'child-training systems' for the 'desirable' development of children.[13] If parents cannot provide a firm footing or are unable to 'break the chain', then others must do it for them! We cannot stand idly

---

12 One of the fairy tales written by the brothers Grimm.
13 Erik Erikson, *Childhood and Society*, 372-3.

by while countless children are churned out, scarred for life. This will not do; we are better than that. What many adults overlook, consciously or not, is that children do cry out. Sometimes loudly, but more often muted in the painful sound of silence. If we fail to pick up these signals, we fail our children. And time is not on our side. Children grow up quickly and soon leave the nest. We must start now before it gets too late, as in the case of young offenders.

I was just sixteen when I flew the nest, well, almost seventeen. I couldn't wait to leave; there was nothing at home to make me stay. School results were disappointing; I'd lost interest. A music career too, like history before that, no longer appealed. I did consider going into graphic design (drawing was another little talent I had discovered), and my poor father even got me enrolled at Art School, but when I saw the same names doing all the illustrations in various magazines, I thought, *there's no room for me* (where have I heard that before?). At that time, I had just started playing golf via lessons from school. The pro who had given us the lessons was starting up on his own near London and was looking for an assistant. Was I interested? Yes, please! I jumped at the opportunity and said farewell. If I had any feelings of guilt, it was towards my younger brother. It felt like deserting him and leaving him to his own fate, snakes and all! Some years later, I confessed this and asked him for forgiveness. Which he gave, god bless him. He understood more than I gave him credit for. Thankfully, it has not spoiled our relationship but possibly brought us closer together.

So, now I had broken free, I was on my own. Yet as the discerning reader knows, I was not happy. I had fled home to escape the tension, but the self-doubt and uncertainty remained. Yes, I could now 'go my own way, do my own thing', but what way, what thing? A career in golf? No, that was just me clutching at the first straw that came along. Didn't I know who I was then? Oh yes, now I remember: an Englishman with a shared musical heritage, an urge to travel, a fear of flying, snakes and dogs but not cows *and* an inconclusive education. Now there's a challenge. How to move forwards with such a motley collection of incongruous stimuli that together form the ingredients of my personality!

Once again, the refrain of the Val Doonican song haunts me, such wonderful advice that I wonderfully missed!

Thus, I didn't walk tall but bungled on without firm footing and entrenched myself still further into my retreat as the fool on the hill. What is this fool on the hill thing anyway? You're right; let me explain.

The fool on the hill was my private domain, a refuge from the madding crowd. It seemed a suitable metaphor to fit my sense of being a loner, an outsider. Psychologically, I guess it was the result of my growing up *invisible*. I think it started around eight or nine years of age when, significantly, my sight started to shorten (I didn't like what I saw in the mirror or the world around me!). We first noticed my blurring vision during those games of trying to read the license plates of cars passing by. That was followed by a test at the opticians and a prescription to wear glasses. These I hated – the combination of sticking out ears *and* spectacles, oh dear!

Well, if I needed glasses to see the world, then the world would have to do its best to see me. So, I took to hiding and walking stealthily like an Indian. During outdoor walks I would make it my aim not to be observed and, now and then, 'ambush' my parents by surprise. If they had seen me coming, then I had failed my objective and must try better the next time. Anyway, I was already invisible to them; my mother only had eyes for my father and he in turn only had eyes for his perfection, so I had no idea how to win her love and his admiration. For better or for worse, parents do make an impact.

About a year later we moved and had to adjust to different surroundings: new schools, new friends, new house, new everything… but instead of mixing in and making new friends,

I withdrew into my fantasy world and cultivated my self-image as a loner. It became a sport, observing others and avoiding contact (analysing group behaviour, which I still do today, dates from this obsession!). Well, it had its benefits, like avoiding being chosen for a mundane or ridiculous task or being drawn into some stupid game. It even saved my bacon once. One evening, while 'participating' at the local youth club (but not really mixing in), a vicious group of 'skinheads'[14] suddenly descended on us, brandishing chains and knives and threatening to 'beat the hell out of us'. I was outside playing hide-and-seek and just caught a glimpse of them in time to warn others and hide myself. The raiders were fast and swept through the grounds before entering the club building. I put my practised skills to such effect, artfully moving from one tree to another, that they missed me. So, thankfully I came away unscathed while many others were mauled and some even badly hurt.

Benefits aside, I soon discovered that there were also drawbacks. On another occasion, at the same youth club, I was playing hide-and-seek again among the trees. I was so intent on proving my ability to avoid detection that the others just gave up looking for me and went inside, leaving me all alone to smart in my success! I also remember missing out on the Beatles' music, due to my avoiding contact with other schoolmates. After school, one of the boys would invite the others to his house to listen to the latest Beatles song. I could have gone but was too preoccupied with my loner image to give in to the temptation, thus the Beatles passed me by! Of course, I caught up with them some years later, but the opportunity then of sharing the fun, I missed. That really hurt and was perhaps my first wake-up call. Yes, being a loner also means being lonely!

If being lonely was the price to pay for being a loner, then so

---

14 Skinheads was the subculture that emerged in the '60s and owed its name to their short-cropped hair; they also wore military boots and their speciality was holding razzias in nearby towns.

be it. Rather a fool on the hill than a moron in the crowd! This was my defining self-delusion, a buttress to mask my emotional insecurity from myself and from the outer world. Invisible perhaps, invincible certainly not.

Thus, I bungled on, entrenched and alone, observant and castigated, looking for love. I felt drawn towards older, attractive women and there were a few brief relationships, but none were able to 'break the chain'. There was also a very pretty girl of my own age whom I only took out once. I was so ill at ease, almost paralysed, that I didn't have a clue what to do! Who then, would come to my rescue? Tony came; she was the miracle just waiting to happen.

I fell into her arms and blurted out that opening line, "Why can't people love each other?"

She picked me up and broke the chain.

> *'In my heart of hearts, I longed for someone to nestle against.'*
>
> D.H. Lawrence, *The White Peacock*

Chapter Three
Birds of Paradise

Sitting on my hill, under a rather foolish summer hat, is the best place I know to contemplate the world in which we pass our days. Add a bottle of good wine and stimulating company and our search for answers may end right here: in paradise! We find the same idyll recorded a millennium earlier:

'Here with a Loaf of Bread
Beneath the Bough,
A Flask of Wine, a Book of Verse
__and Thou
Beside me singing in the Wilder-
Ness—
And Wilderness is Paradise enow'[15]

Yes, Tony flooded my wilderness with the song of love. She 'laid me down in green pastures and led me besides the still waters'.[16]

---
15   *The Rubáiyát of Omar Khayyám*, Stanza XI (ca 1070 AD).
16   Psalm 23:2.

Being with her was like being in heaven; all was good in our Garden of Eden! God, how I miss her, would that it last forever. Yet even I, the romantic dreamer with a glass too many, must admit that such earthly bliss is but fleeting, even if it does last for forty years! OK yes, happiness may be temporal, but that's no reason to dismiss paradise as an illusion. During our brief sojourn here, we try to comprehend it all. What is life? What is our purpose? Why can't people love each other? So many questions and so few answers. Parents have some, peers and teachers, too. And if we are *lucky*, we may find a fellow traveller to help us on our way.

I found mine in Tony. She took on the Herculean task of restoring my soul. For forty years we battled it out as sparring partners and consummated it as lovers. She in the belief that I would eventually stand on my own two feet. I as an ailing plant, in constant need of 'topping up'.

And it all started on that momentous day in July when she entered our golf shop to book a lesson. Her actual intention, she later told me, was to flirt with some golf pro just to spite her husband. The children were now all grown-up and her marriage was empty and suffocating. She was on holiday with her husband in the New Forest. With time on her hands, golf was a welcome diversion. He was out on the Solent alone for she hated sailing. And, even worse, he had forgotten her birthday. Not even a flower picked from someone's garden! That was the last straw, his downfall, my chance!

So, there we stood on the practice ground on that beautiful summer morning, swaying from one foot to the other like two birds of paradise in the ritual act of mating. An hour must have passed by without hitting a single ball. In fact, Brian, my boss, became so concerned (or just curious), that he sent his younger brother out to see if we were alright. I shall never forget the expression on his face as he approached, from an initial look of concern to one of relieved bemusement on witnessing our clear-for-all-to-see behaviour, and his awkward withdrawal in his hurry to report back! Only recently did I ask him *what* he actually reported. The exact words he'd forgotten but something like, "Brian, I don't think we need worry about them!"

Back on the practice ground, any prospect Tony may have had of a casual flirtation was dashed when I blurted out my opening line. *Just my luck*, she thought. *Instead of a fling with some unsuspecting golf pro, I meet a serious one*. She told me later that that was actually what went through her mind at the time. Anyway, she responded with an introduction to psychology, and it was soon obvious that this was turning into something more than just a 'flirtation'.

During the following days, we met frequently. Sometimes to actually play some golf, more often to lunch or just sit on the rocks, looking out to sea and enjoying the exhilaration of being together. She would ruffle her hand through my hair (it was longer in those days) which provoked my Pavlovian response, "I like that," hoping she would continue![17]

Once, she pointed out a yacht that was sailing by. "That's my husband," she said.

"He might see us."

I replied, "Or should we wave?"

She laughed but shrugged her shoulders and didn't seem to care. On another occasion, again on the rocks, she was lost in thought and then complained about her daughter who had just married a professor, some thirty years older. Now here she was, romancing with a guy thirty years younger and was struck by the irony. I asked if they were happy, which took her by surprise.

"Goh," she said. "I'm so full of my own situation that I didn't even think of that; yes, of course, you're right – I think they are."

The exclamation 'Goh' needs clarification because it is key to understanding her personality. (Pronounced with a soft guttural 'g' as in loch, its closest translation in English is 'gosh'.) She used

---

17 This later became a catch phrase which we always laughed at!

this word daily but always in a *genuine* way and never feigned. It was her stock response to many situations, a spontaneous reaction and *childlike* in character. It was this last quality in particular that set her apart from other adults. I have never met another person, male or female, who possessed this quality to the same degree. Whenever surprised, her eyes and mouth would open wide and the magic word 'Goh' would tumble out, with such disarming effect that even the most hardened of souls would soften!

I remember just one such occasion. It was at a hotel on the south coast where we were staying, whose name I shan't mention. We took breakfast downstairs. The food was excellent. I indulged in a full English; Tony had a continental. The bread rolls, which she loved, were fresh and delicious but, on this occasion, proved her undoing.

"These are so nice," she said. "I think I'll take one for later." She placed her handbag on her lap, opened it, wrapped a bread roll into her used paper serviette and put the contents into her bag. All quite naturally and without ceremony.

Now, the 'hoarding' of articles of food from a hotel breakfast room, as if it were an unlimited self-service, is met with mixed approval. Many do it, and this was the only time I've seen Tony do it, too! In some establishments it is simply 'not done', in others frowned upon, while others just turn a blind eye or show indifference. Whatever the case, in cannot be said to be actively encouraged. I've yet to see the sign 'please take as much as you like – we'll provide a doggy bag'!

Back in the breakfast room. Tony had barely placed the bread roll into her handbag when a waitress suddenly descended upon her like a bat out of hell and promptly removed all the silver cutlery, curtly remarking, "Before you take these as well." The waitress in question was the most unfriendly person thinkable. Menacing, grim and unaccommodating, completely unsuitable for the position she held and in stark contrast with the food that was served. Customer *un*friendly, without any doubt. Tony's reaction, as the reader has already guessed, was her classic "Goh!"

At first, the waitress seemed unmoved. She turned to leave, nose in the air and with an implacable expression. Then she appeared to hesitate, only momentarily, while her mouth turned into a little wry grin. No discussion followed, no further reprimand, just a wry grin. That was as far as she would go. Beneath that hard exterior lurked a human being and Tony's 'Goh' had triggered a miniscule meltdown!

Childlike innocence is a thing of beauty: so heart-warming in young children and so tragic seeing them lose it as they grow older. It is a consequence of growing up we say, as if to justify adulthood. One day while shopping, I saw a little boy jumping up and down in excitement and pointing up to the sky. "Look, Mummy, an aeroplane!" he cried.

"That's not an *aeroplane*, stupid; that's a hel-i-cop-ter," she replied in the most stern and impatient manner she could muster. The little boy stopped jumping up and down. Great job, Mum, well done! You've dampened his enthusiasm, corrected his 'mistake', called him stupid and spoilt his day – another kid bites the dust, mission accomplished! And all the passers-by just passed by and didn't say a word, me included!

That was many years ago. Now, I would speak up because parents do struggle, and children suffer. They all deserve better. We are in such a hurry to get our kids to grow up and to become like us: world-wise adults who claim to know it all. Just stop and reflect on this. Look at Van Gogh's painting *Child with an Orange* (1890). The little girl is portrayed as a 'miniature adult' as if to imply that 'as members of the banal adult world, we are tragically denied the hidden secrets of youth forever'.[18] Beware of innocence lost, for it leads to corruption of the soul. I guess this

---

18 Josephine Cutts and James Smith, *Van Gogh* (Bath, 2002), 242.

is why only those who have 'become as little children' will 'enter into the kingdom of heaven'.[19]

But here in paradise, not all adults lose their innocence, as Tony shows. *She*, the social scientist would say, is the negative instance. The exception that disproves the hypothesis. We may put this down to her being a 'thriving plant'. She is blessed with having paradise on her doorstep! Does this mean that healthy plants need not look far for answers? Is a firm footing alone enough for contentment and purpose in life? And what about the others? How do *they* cope and become as little children? For the broken plant, *hell* is the reality, not heaven; for the ailing plant too, there's little fun to be had in this world – Eldorado seems far away. It reminds me of a Cat Stevens song, 'Wild World',[20] which exhorts putting on a brave face in order to cope with the world.

In throwing myself at Tony's feet I put, as it were, all my eggs in one basket. I entrusted her to untangle my spiritual turmoil. I was not wrong, but what did she see in me? Did she really expect our relationship to work? Initially, many of her friends and relatives looked askance at her dalliance with a much younger man. 'Baby-snatching' it was called! She was being vain and selfish *and* unfair in denying me a 'normal' life. And who was I, anyway, to break up a long-standing marriage?

This was not lost on Tony. She did have her doubts. But not about her marriage; as far as she was concerned, that was over already. No, she had *financial* qualms about leaving the security of a well-established home and worries about how her children would react. Also, did I *really* love her or was this just a 'mother-fixation' thing on my side (she was well-versed in Freudian psychology).

These aspects did preoccupy our first years together and, at times, threatened our relationship. Before definitely deciding on a life together, she wanted the assurance that I loved her *for herself*

---

19   Mathew 18:3.
20   Cat Stevens, *Wild World* (1970).

and not (only) as a substitute mother. This I couldn't give, for I was an emotional knot. What did I really know about my own motives? And yes, in a sense she *did* replace my mother, though we both felt that our love was more than just that.[21] Give me a substitute mother like Tony any day! Anyway, I took therapy for two years, which helped gain a surer footing and clearer understanding of where we stood. During this period, Tony introduced me to the ideas of Freud, Jung, Fromm, Maslow, Piaget, Erikson and others, which were eye-openers to me and provided answers to many questions.

So, why were we attracted to each other? What subtle chemistry was involved in the forging of our destiny? These are difficult questions to answer. At first glance, we seemed poles apart. Not just in age but also in outlook. Me an outsider, moving away from people, Tony an insider moving towards people. She on the inside looking out, me on the outside looking in. She self-confident and at ease with the world, I self-doubting and at war with the world. She the thriving plant, me the ailing one. Yet despite these differences, we instinctively recognised each other as two complementary halves of a symbiotic whole. Two sides of one coin. Yes, I think that's a fair assessment. We both shared the same yearning to understand human nature and struggled with the same questions, albeit from our own viewpoint. Or perhaps we were just 'struck by lightning', as Simone Signoret said on meeting Yves Montand in St Paul de Vence in 1949.[22] I like that too!

The months prior to our first meeting had been stressful for Tony. Her mother had just died and, as an only child, she had the inheritance to settle. Her youngest son was at the point of leaving home and looking for appropriate student accommodation, leaving Mum the prospect of an empty house and an empty

---

21 My mother sometimes made a *Freudian* slip of the tongue when referring to Tony as *your mother*!
22 Ted Jones, The French Riviera (London, 2007), 98.

marriage. On top of that, she had undergone a precautionary operation (removal of the uterus) to reduce a potential risk of cancer. After meeting me, she deeply regretted having had that operation. She would have loved to have another child, with me as the father! Fate, it would seem, was playing its devious hand.

Moreover, during her recovery from the operation, a friend of hers gave her a book to read. Whether from uncanny foresight or just coincidence, I cannot say, but the impact was huge. It struck a chord with Tony's heart at precisely the right moment. The book tells the story of a middle-aged woman's second chance. 'Her husband is away for the summer. Her grown-up children have scattered. Suddenly a glamorous career and a young lover beckon her to an exciting future'.[23] Tony devoured its content, underlining many passages and adding numerous remarks. Just three months later, fiction turns into fact and I become her 'second chance'. Now, tell me you don't believe in fate!

On the subject of fiction, the first two years of our romance do contain some elements worthy of a romantic novel. Countless letters to and fro, clandestine meetings, secret liaisons in hotel rooms, all precursors to the great adventure that we were about to embark on. And the great leap on my part began with a misunderstanding!

Tony invited me to come and stay in the Netherlands for a week's holiday. She had sent me some money for the trip and would pick me up at the airport. This prospect took my breath away. I needed no further prompting, and, in my delirium, I left my job, terminated my lodgings, packed *all* my bags, including my large golf bag, and said farewell to England… the things we do for love!

Thus, I arrived at Amsterdam airport full of anticipation and excitement, but where was Tony? I waited and waited but she didn't show up. Had I got it wrong? She did say the airport or

---

23   Doris Lessing, *The Summer Before the Dark* (New York, 1973).

was it the station? No, I still had her letter and it was definitely the airport. What to do? There were no mobile phones back then, but I did have their home address. It was in the southern part of the Netherlands, in fact, just over the border into Belgium. All very intense for a young guy in his early twenties whose only other trip to Europe was a school holiday seven years ago! This was now for real.

From her letters, I remembered her saying that Eindhoven was the nearest large town to where they lived. So, I bought a single train ticket to Eindhoven, hauled all my baggage on board and set off into the sun. Getting off at Eindhoven, I started to look for Tony again. After another long wait (it was probably quite short, but it seemed very long), I decided to take a taxi to their home address as I had no idea how to get there otherwise. I was sensible enough to ask the price first, just in case I didn't have enough on me.

After about thirty minutes, the taxi crossed the border into Belgium and shortly arrived at the address I had given. It was a nice residential area consisting of spacious bungalows set among pine trees. I later learnt that many Dutch families had settled there for tax reasons. The taxi stopped in front of their home. I had a clear view of the living room and saw her husband wielding a 'Swing-Rite' (a practice golf club with an adjustable weight at the end) but I didn't see her, or her car parked outside. This didn't feel right. Where was she and did he know about my coming, surely not. The taxi driver, sensing my hesitation, asked if this was the right address. Yes, I said, but I'd changed my mind and could he please take me to the nearest hotel.

"As it happens," he said, "there's one just back on the main road; I'll take you there."

So, I booked a room at this hotel which, unknown to me, was of ill-repute. I'll refrain from using the word 'brothel', but the reader will get my drift. Anyway, it was just for one night and time to consider my options. Where had it all gone wrong?

In the morning, with no answers and much foreboding, I took my breakfast in that disreputable hotel and sat at the window, looking gloomily out onto the main road, still wondering what to do. At that moment, a car passed by and I recognised the driver, no not Tony but her husband, no doubt off to work. This was my chance. I asked if I could leave my baggage there and pick it up later.

"Of course," the lady in charge said.

So, I set off in the direction of their home, hoping to find Tony there. She was not. No sign of any movement, no car outside. What now? Well, I couldn't just hang around until someone showed up; that might take ages. And what if her husband returned, that wouldn't do either! Possibly, the neighbours had already seen me lurking around and might soon call the police. There was only one solution, as I then saw it, and that was to confide in the neighbours, but which ones? Who was to be trusted with this delicate situation, the neighbours to the left or the ones on the right? Who was most likely to be sympathetic to Tony's cause?

My intuition came to the rescue. I opted for the neighbours to the left. The couple on the right were older and seemed to me a little conservative. On the left, I caught a glimpse of a woman about Tony's age. *Try her*, I thought and yes, I struck gold! She took me in, listened to my story and proposed a plan of action. She would take me to the Eindhoven Golf Club. Tony was a member there and it was a natural place for me to wait. In the meantime, she would try to contact Tony and let her know where I was. I trusted her wisdom and let events unfold. I remember playing a hole or two, just to pass the time, but neither my head nor heart was in the game. All I wanted was to be reunited with Tony. At last, after much restless waiting, Tony entered the clubhouse and took me back out to her car amidst a profusion of mutual apologies!

Now, the reader is dying to know, like me, what went wrong. Tony had indeed waited for me at the airport, i.e. *Eindhoven* airport, not Amsterdam! A colossal misunderstanding, with momentous repercussions. After the airport, she had intended to take me to her new apartment on the coast, where we could be together.[24] All this under the pretext of spending a few days with her cousin! That was the plan. Now things had changed. This scheme had to be abandoned and there was no plan B. We were longing to lie in each other's arms but had nowhere to go. Resourceful as ever, Tony adopted a desperate measure. Now your presence here is known, she argued, then you must come and stay with us as my guest, under the same roof as her husband! Well, Reader, I did warn you that this was a romantic novel!

At first, this bold and daring solution seemed to work. He took it, I must say, quite graciously. But as the days turned into weeks, the pretence of a holiday visit was no longer tenable. I admitted that I thought of giving up golf altogether and trying my hand at something else here in the Netherlands. How else could I explain my prolonged stay and excess baggage? We considered a number of possibilities from truck driver to helicopter pilot and he even helped me find some contacts. Whether out of real concern for my welfare or just his way of getting rid of me, I can't say. In his place, I would have thrown me out long ago! Anyway, the tension was mounting, and arguments followed. Things were coming to a head. Tony got me out of the house and found me accommodation at a friend's house. We said that I had gone back to England, just to let tempers cool down.

During the ensuing months, I found temporary work and we saw each other whenever we could. It was a difficult period for all parties. Then, fate struck again. I got a call from my former boss, Brian (who has since become my life-long friend), begging me to come back and help run his business with his younger brother. Why? He had unfortunately been diagnosed with Hodgkin's, a lymphatic disease. The prescribed treatment of radiotherapy was intensive

---

24 Bought from the money she had recently inherited, it became our love nest for the next forty years!

and meant him being out of the picture for at least six months. Poor chap and poor me – another dilemma! While he was there fighting for his life, I was here fighting for a life with Tony. What to do? Tony and I had a long, emotional talk. I decided to throw the glove in the ring. "I'm going back to help Brian but *only* if you come with me," I said, and to underline my resolve I went out and sat cross-legged on the lawn! Now it was her turn to take a leap of faith into the unknown. Which she did. My beloved Tony said *yes*!

Thank you, Brian, for that! It all started with you. It was you who *brought* us together. When Tony first entered your shop, you wanted to give the lessons but decided to give me the opportunity instead. How can I ever thank you for that? Now, it was you who *joined* us together. In requesting my help, you inadvertently threw us a lifeline. It was just what we needed at that moment. It forced our hand and precipitated a life commitment. Of course, there were also other factors. Her youngest son had, in the meantime, found student accommodation and was at the point of moving out. Whatever happened, she had always said that she would wait until he was settled. That was important to her. Neither could she see a way back to her former life, especially now there was open hostility with her husband. Moreover, our attachment to each other was growing daily and could no longer be ignored. It was her choice and what a courageous one! To burn all her bridges behind her and set off with a young man into an uncertain future, wow, now it was my turn to say 'Goh'! Later, when we were more settled, many of her friends and family, who were sceptical at the time, not only came to visit us but also praised her courage and admitted being envious of her adaptability. She was an example of how to take a 'second chance' when it presented itself!

To return to the question that preoccupied us both. *How* do ailing plants cope? Do they have any chance of a glimpse or share of paradise? Statistically, the odds are stacked against them. They are too many and there are simply not enough thriving plants to go around. Scientific evidence to support this sweeping statement is lacking because this ratio, or approach, has yet to be researched. Besides, this is not a scientific study, we are but reflecting. My instinct tells me however, that this view *is* historically sound.

Tony was convinced that what they lacked was a firm footing and that this could be given freely, through loving care and attention. Yes, but the only trouble here is that *love* is the deciding factor, and this can only be given freely in a one-to-one relationship. Unless you're a saint like Mother Theresa, there is simply not enough love to go round! Thus, a thriving plant may be able to help a number of ailing plants through loving care and attention but is unable to give love to them *all*. This begs the question: just how many neglected plants are actually saved? How many are subsequently able to stand on their own two feet and find purpose and contentment? The answer to this may reveal our own stance in life: optimistic or pessimistic. Perhaps the treatment *can* be improved, or perhaps it doesn't matter. Is not the saving of just *one* soul the most important thing?

And what is our definition of a 'thriving plant' anyway? Possibly, many of us would describe ourselves as thriving and normal, inferring that the number of 'ailing plants' are not a majority at all but the very opposite – a sad minority! Well, in that case, why aren't we doing more to help them, indeed, why are there so many obviously struggling to get by? Do you not see them? Or are you taken in by their smiles? He who looks into a mirror sees he not himself?

If any of this makes sense, we can distinguish between ailing plants that have received care and attention, and those that have *also* received love. Arguably, the latter have more chance of getting a good share of paradise, while the former will have to make do with a tantalising glimpse, like a yearly two-week holiday on a tropical island! If this sounds familiar, then you know what sort you belong to. Welcome to paradise!

> *'What is man, that thou art mindful of him?'*
>
> The Bible, Psalm VIII:4

Chapter Four
Lost in Paradise

On my foolish hill in paradise, I recall the lines of the Beatles' song.[25] Then Tony wakes me up and says that I am dreaming, or rather that I'm the 'dreamer', as sung by Supertramp.[26] She says that I suffer, like many young people, from what the Germans call *Weltschmerz*. This is not a medical condition but rather a state of mind connected with growing up. (Webster's Dictionary defines it as 'mental depression or apathy caused by comparison of the actual state of the world with an ideal state', and in romantic literature it is often expressed as a mood of sentimental sadness.) Coming to terms with the physical and mental changes involved with adulthood can be very disorientating for adolescents. This is an intense period full of self-doubt, psychological introspection and realignment *and* often involving a search for meaning, outside oneself. The

---

25 J. Lennon/P. McCartney, *The Fool on the Hill* (1967). As promised, I didn't miss out entirely on the Beatles!
26 R. Davies/R. Hodgson, *Dreamer* (1974). A hit song by the band, Supertramp.

nature of any suffering that may accompany this process is existential, for it concerns the individual and his or her place in the world.

In primitive societies, the transition from childhood to adulthood is celebrated through a ritual of initiation. Known as 'rites of passage', such ceremonies frequently involve physical pain – breaking of teeth, piercing of flesh and tattooing – for it is understood that the necessity and endurance of pain is a hallmark of adulthood. In modern society, vestiges of this custom are still found in the initiation ceremonies of certain gangs, clubs and schools. The original function of initiation, however, has long since disappeared, leaving the youth, as it were, to fend for itself. As one psychoanalyst has put it:

'... the individual, thrust upon his own resources, is and feels unprotected. The general feeling of insecurity is increased by the fact that for the most part neither tradition nor religion is strong enough *today* to give the individual a feeling of being an integral part of a more powerful unity, providing shelter and directing his strivings'.[27] [Italics added.]

With our sights set on civilisation, we highlight what we have gained and forget to measure it against what we have lost! This, arguably, is a major aspect of the phenomenon, *Weltschmerz*. Though now, I am getting ahead of myself.

Tony suggested we start by examining my *psychological* need to be a fool on the hill. We found it was closely connected with a feeling of 'emotional isolation' and my resulting desire to 'move away from people'. The fool on the hill was my 'idealised image',[28] a safe haven where no one could touch me, as poetically described in the Simon & Garfunkel song.[29] I went into therapy, which helped unravel the emotional knot and lure me out of my

---

27 Karen Horney, *New Ways in Psychoanalysis*, 174.
28 Karen Horney, *Our Inner Conflicts*, Chapter Six deals with this concept in detail.
29 P. Simon/A. Garfunkel, *I am a Rock* (1965).

self-imposed isolation. Slowly, I adjusted to the idea that 'moving towards people' wasn't so frightening, after all.

At a social gathering or reception, Tony was always relaxed and struck up conversation easily.

"How do you do it?" I asked.

"Well," she said, "if you look closely, you will see that most people *appear* to be enjoying themselves, but in fact they are *not*. They laugh too loud, drink too much and form little groups among those they already know. And there are always a few, like yourself, who stand alone and look a little lost. My advice is to go straight up to one of those and say something stupid like, 'I hate these sorts of gatherings, don't you?' or, 'you look like the sort of person who can tell me what's going on here!'. It doesn't really matter *what* you say but that you say it to someone who is *waiting to be spoken to*. This will prompt a response and a conversation will naturally follow. You may even get on like a house on fire!"

This approach, I should add, suited me as a fool on the hill. Tony realised that this was my chosen habitat, my comfort zone, and had no wish to change it. She *could* have told me to join in with the groups but deliberately steered me towards other 'outsiders'.

I put this advice to the test and found it always worked. Admittedly it didn't always click with the person chosen, but in that case, I just chose someone else! In mastering how to move towards people, I was overcoming my emotional fear of social intercourse. This was Tony's aim. She wanted me to become mentally stronger and more self-confident. Agreed, but I was *not* going to give up my stance as an outsider. No way! I've never moved with the crowd, never shall and never will. In short, Tony helped me discard the *negative* psychological baggage I had filled my fool-on-the-hill image with. What remained was a social space where my personality could develop. Whoopee!

If I complained about the stupidity of people and finding it difficult to mix in, Tony also admitted how annoying some of them could be and that she was sometimes at a loss how to shake them off.

"Why is it," she sighed, "that the *awful* types always seem attracted to me?"

Now it was my turn to give advice. That, I said, is because you're a *rose on the dunghill*. That is your strength and your fate! Her reaction was a lovely, 'Goh'!

Despite our different standpoints, me outside looking in and she inside looking out, we shared common ground: observing people and analysing behaviour. Proud of my helicopter view, I thought I alone was able to see what the crowd could not. Tony proved me wrong. Situated in the middle of the stream as it were, she was ideally placed to observe everything that was going on around her. Her firm footing enabled her to stand her ground, like a rock that is *not* borne along by the current. She was *in* the crowded river but impervious to its insistent drag. As in the centre of a storm where all is calm, she serenely watched the world go whirling by – round and round and round! Later, when I fully appreciated her position, I understood her attraction to the 'hustle and bustle', as she called it. I, who hated the throng of the multitude, found this difficult to swallow, until I saw how calm, and even indifferent she was towards it. Tony enjoyed the daily buzz of activity for what it was, precisely because it *didn't* affect her inner self.

And it was precisely this, that caused unwanted flotsam to gravitate towards her peaceful station and lodge itself, reluctant to move on, like drowning souls clinging to the wreckage. Which is what they were. Ailing plants with no one to tend them. I should know, I was one of them! But at least I was young. Many of the ailing plants Tony complained of were older and probably beyond repair. Once they pass a certain age, she said, usually twenty-five to thirty, they are unlikely to change. They get stuck in their ways or haven't yet found a stabilising relationship.

Without a major upheaval, their ailment (behaviour) takes root and defines their character. Not so with the young. They still feel their pain and cry out, hopeful that someone will help. This is why Tony focused on children and adolescents. They can be saved. They must be saved, before it is too late. Before they end up as damaged goods and no longer conscious of their pain.

No, it was the *awful* ones, as she called them, who would knock on her door, who she found difficult to shake off. Like leeches on a healthy plant, they would attach themselves and sap out her living energy. Relentless in their constant need of attention and wailing for recognition, their very presence was enough to exhaust and drain the host if she proves unarmed. And Tony was unarmed. Under normal circumstances and among not too injured plants, her open and warm nature was always effective and disarming. These hardened creatures, however, were another kettle of fish!

They had become accustomed to rebuttal. Others kept well clear of them, relying on a sixth sense to keep them away from danger. For the awful ones, this meant that whoever they might turn to seemed controlled by the law of diminishing returns and were forever evaporating! And the harder they tried, the more the others disappeared. Except for Tony. She stood her ground. Unsuspecting and self-possessed, she welcomed all with open arms. But these creatures, surprised at this show of hospitality and flattered by its sincerity, were yet wily and well-versed in disguise and *hid* their inner selves in the hope of prolonging their stay. But, as irony would have it, in overstaying their welcome, which they invariably did, they revealed precisely that side of their character they were trying to hide! Yes, as Tony found out, once a leech has got hold, it will not easily be shaken off.

After being initially taken in by their charms or tales of woe, Tony suffered the ensuing fatigue and felt defenceless. Hints and well-meant advice, effective with others, fell here on stony ground. They were simply *too* bossy, *too* overbearing, *too* fussy, *too* rigid, *too* nervous, *too* whatever the case. These poor souls really were beyond repair. I explained to Tony that they were attracted to her because no one else could stomach them, while she at least gave them a hearing. She tried sterner measures, including mockery – her most formidable weapon – avoidance, not answering the phone, and even pushing them out of the door, but still they kept trying to worm themselves into her favour! She then agreed they were too far gone, pathological specimens, and that further contact was pointless. One by one, she gave them up, disappointed, but with a huge sigh of relief!

Her paradise was warm and serene, and she enjoyed every minute of it. Now and then, some lost soul would indeed wash ashore and bask on her sunny beach, perhaps still looking for paradise and unable to find it. An awful one could disturb the serenity but never succeed in grasping it.

From the centre of her self-supporting universe, Tony looked out and observed people with the eye of an artist. In fact, she drew and painted remarkably well: people, animals and landscapes or whatever took her fancy. With a childlike fascination, she was often absorbed in capturing a scene in her drawing book or on whatever paper was at hand. Anything would do, from the back of a beer mat to a torn off piece of newspaper. She was always drawing something. Faces were her favourite and often as caricatures with cartoon captions, which reminds me of the lovers on the bus in the Simon & Garfunkel song,[30] such fun and so young at heart! And when she wasn't drawing, she was writing. Again, on anything at hand and ranging from poetry and ideas she thought worth noting, to a mundane shopping list or the name of someone she had to call. So engaged and self-sufficient, like a child absorbed in play, impossible to disturb!

It was these qualities, serenity *and* the observant eye of an artist, that enabled her to fathom out people and get straight

---

30 P. Simon/A. Garfunkel, *America* (1965).

to the heart of things. One day, Tony was chatting with her university friends, whom I shall call Ida and Wilma. The topic was men and marriage (surprise!). Wilma was intimating at not being happy with her husband and asked Tony what she thought of him.

Without giving it a second thought, she replied, "A charming despot," to which Ida exclaimed, "Oh my!" and all three began to giggle like girls do when discussing a sensitive subject.

"Yes," Wilma responded, after the giggling had subsided, "that's him in a nutshell!"

On another occasion, in the golf shop, a customer who was also a club member entered, and I went out to help him. Tony was in the back room and could only hear our voices.

After he had left, she came out and said, "What a dishonest man that was."

"How do you know that?" I asked. "You didn't see him, and you've never met him before."

"No," she said, "but I could hear the way he talked; that was enough." Tony explained that you could always tell whether a person was honest, either by looking at their eyes or listening to their voice. And not so much *what* they said but *how* they said it! This, I suppose, is why men and women who fail to make this distinction get duped and fall for such 'smooth operators'!

Needless to say, she was right! Brian and I had for some time suspected this particular member of stealing things from the shop. Now we were on to him and hoped to catch him red-handed. A few days later, I saw him leave the shop with a golf club tucked under his arm. Brian, being away and fearing the worst, told me to call him if something happened. I did, and I asked him what I should do. Was I sure? Yes. Then we must act quickly, before he gets the stolen item from his locker to the car. I was to keep an eye on the locker, while Brian called the police and club secretary. The member was apprehended, but he turned out to be more of a kleptomaniac than an ordinary thief. He couldn't help himself, as his locker, still full of his hoard, bore witness! He was also one of the richer club members and a respectable 'pillar of the community'. Did we really wish to take this matter to court? After consideration, yes, we did. Sure, he did return the goods in his locker (he had no choice), he did offer Brian compensation (not enough by far) and promised to be a good boy in the future. But his dishonesty spoke against him. He not only took goods from the shop but also cheated on the course. He was not generally liked, and many wanted to see the back of him. So yes, we took him to court.

I still have the sketches Tony made during the trial, with their cartoon quality and humorous captions. How she drew the prosecutor with penetrating eyes and pointed nose, while he made mincemeat of me in the witness stand – was I sure that the club I had seen him leave the shop with was the exact same item that he had stolen? (Caption reads: poor witness, confused and bewildered.) How she portrayed the defendant with shifty eyes and defiant glare in the knowledge that he, a respectable citizen, was *not* going to be sentenced. (Caption reads: defendant gloating.) How absurd to be pilloried just on the flimsy evidence of a couple of youngsters! And so it was, our case didn't stand. We were unable to establish the *exact* identity of the stolen item. And, even though more stolen goods were found at his home from *other* pro-shops in the area, he was acquitted. A big blow for justice, very disheartening, but on the upside, he did leave the club and we never saw him again!

It is disconcerting, the myriad of *awful* ones ageing here in paradise: kleptomaniacs, perverts, idiots, pathological liars, thieves and cut-throats. Quite a motley crew, who give us plenty to talk about and reflect upon. Colourful as they are, this group, thankfully, is but a minority. A small portion of mankind we can hopefully entrust to the care of specialists, to deal with as they see fit. As for the rest, the less severe cases like myself, I suggest their number is considerable, for if Tony is anything to go by, the *healthy* plants seem equally few and far between. In other words, though we have few statistics to go by, the number of plants found ailing on the spectrum, between the broken and the healthy, is by far the largest. Their ailments vary from a mild cold to a severe case of influenza and treatment from a quick cure (one aspirin tablet) to intensive care (incarceration). Yet, they all share one thing in common: the desire to be healthy, happy and blessed.

Their pain however, whatever the degree of severity, is not physical but *existential*. It relates to family upbringing, genetic make-up and social environment, a deficiency or mismatch in one or more of these areas. They strive for paradise but are lost and unable to find it. Their view of life is negative, and they struggle to find any meaning. *Weltschmerz*: I am sick; the world is sick. Individual treatment can help, but more often the pain is projected onto the external world, resulting in a pessimistic worldview. Like atheists who struggle with faith and turn away from God.

But their complaints are not to be passed off as just the groaning of the sick. They are very real, and often make a valid point. Have *we* given them enough love and attention? Have *we* shown a positive attitude towards life? Do *we* know who we are? Is *our* social environment meaningful? Their despair makes us feel uncomfortable, and all too often we turn a blind eye. It requires strength to confront the issues and show concern, for that involves looking into the mirror. Is it our fault they are suffering? If anyone is to blame, perhaps it is God!

The magnitude of the cry of the ailing, from sheer numbers, is great. It speaks to the world for all to hear. Evidence of this is not to be found in statistics, but, for example, in the collective mass of literary observation. Here, we have a fully documented, suggestive and fascinating opus to reflect upon. The sum of authors disseminating their views appears endless and could easily fill a volume. And is not restricted to *modern* literature alone but stretches back to the earliest written records. By way of illustration, allow me, Dear Reader, to overload you with a few choice extracts.

In his last great novel, *Resurrection*, Tolstoy paints the following scene on the very opening page:

'Though men in their hundreds of thousands had tried their hardest to disfigure that little corner of the earth where they had crowded themselves together, paving the ground with stones so that nothing could grow, [...] spring, however, was still spring, even in the town. [...] All were happy – plants, birds, insects and children. But grown-up people – adult men and women – never left off cheating and tormenting themselves and one another. [...] No, what they considered sacred and important were their own devices for wielding power over each other'.[31]

The picture of adults 'cheating and tormenting themselves' is, for Tolstoy, an evident truth and a deliberate generalisation. As if to say, this is the condition of man – escape it if you can! On the final page of William Golding's novel *Lord of the Flies*, we find Ralph, the chief character, weeping for the 'end of innocence, the darkness of man's heart'. And in *Women in Love*, D.H. Lawrence considers humanity a 'dead letter', to be done away with altogether:

'The whole idea is dead. Humanity is dry-rotten, really. There are myriads of human beings hanging on the bush – and they look very nice and rosy, your healthy young men and women. But they are apples of Sodom, as a matter of fact, Dead Sea Fruit, gall-apples. It isn't true that they have any significance – their insides are full of bitter, corrupt ash". "But there *are* good people", protested Ursula. "Good enough for the life of today. But mankind is a dead tree, covered with fine brilliant galls of people'.[32]

Further back in time, the political philosopher, Thomas Hobbes, stated that since his banishment from the Garden of

---

31   *Resurrection*, 19.
32   *Women in Love*, 65, 140.

Eden, man's existence has become 'short, nasty and brutish'.[33] While Pascal, his contemporary, adds, 'being unable to cure death, wretchedness and ignorance, men have decided, in order to be happy, not to think about such things' and seek instead 'diversion and occupation' as a 'result of their constant sense of wretchedness'.[34]

And still further back, we find that doleful Persian poet delighting us with a quatrain of singular wishful thinking:

'Ah, Love! Could thou and I
With Fate conspire
To grasp this sorry Scheme of
Things entire,
Would not we shatter it to bits –
And then
Re-mould it nearer to the Heart's
Desire?'[35]

In the *Bible*, which is saturated with references to man's misery and insignificance, we find Job complaining, 'What is man, that thou shouldest magnify him?'. Job is told to 'enquire [...] of the former age, and prepare thyself to the search of their fathers, For, we are *but of yesterday, and know nothing, because our days upon earth are a shadow*'.[36] [Italics added.] And even Moses, that great man of God, is not found wanting:

'Thou hast set our iniquities before thee, our secret sins in the light of thy countenance. For all our days are passed away in thy wrath: we spend our years as a tale that is told. The days of our years are threescore years and ten; and if by reason of strength

---

33 Thomas Hobbes, *Leviathan* (1st publ. 1651, London, 1937), 65. (For the full quote and context, see chapter 13.)
34 Blaise Pascal, *Pensées*, 66–69.
35 *Rubáiyát of Omar Khayyám*, Stanza LXXIII.
36 *Job*, VII, 17 and VIII, 8–9.

they be fourscore years, yet is their strength labour and sorrow; for it is soon cut off, and we fly away'.[37]

Taken together, all this gloom does not augur well with a more optimistic view of mankind. As for paradise, well, this must be written off as a laughable illusion. God has, after all, thrown us out! In the face of this damning literary evidence and such a reservoir of pessimism, the conclusion that this is a natural expression of humanity, seems justified. With so many ailing plants, a bleak outlook on life is inevitable. *C'est la vie!*

If literature's contribution seems disappointing, perhaps philosophy or science can shed a more benevolent light. But no, here too, our hopes are dashed. So many philosophers, in particular the existentialists, have undertaken an enquiry into the 'existentialism of being', only to end in nihilism and despair. To paraphrase one author, 'existentialism was a philosophy of man without an organised religion, though not necessarily without God. Here man is free, but the world is empty and meaningless... there is nothing further to be done'.[38]

Science, too, fares little better. According to one historiographer, 'mountains of theory' have been built in our attempt to understand human history. Much of these, he argues, are 'castles in the air', for 'we know next to nothing... have only the haziest of notions... there is next to no evidence to go by'. Faced with this 'curtain of silence' that 'shrouds tens of thousands of years', it is better to 'admit our ignorance' and accept that 'cautious generalisations are about as far as we can go'.[39] Coming from an empirical scientist trained to accept only truths proven by verifiable facts, this challenge to the scientific community sounds more like a loss of faith, significantly witnessed, perhaps, by the author's 'flirt' with Buddhism in the final pages of this much acclaimed book!

---

37 *Psalm* XC, 8–10.
38 Colin Wilson, *The New Existentialism*, 32–33.
39 Yuval Noah Harari, *Sapiens: A Brief History of Humankind*, 62–68.

In short, through the ages, from the *Bible* to present-day thinkers, from poets to philosophers, artists and scientists, all have found occasion to dishearten their readers with their despairing take on life! On the strength of their numbers alone, are they to have the last word? No, we can't accept that. We must somehow lighten their load. Perhaps even turn their sorrow into joy! Besides, we're still in paradise are we not, or are we irrevocably lost, after all?

This is a good moment to remind myself not to get *too* embroiled in metaphysical speculation. The purpose of this book was to *reflect* on the meaning of life, with a sense of fun true to Tony's spirit. Yes, of course, we speculated too, but even on serious subjects, we never took ourselves *too* seriously. Once, while discussing the origin of man, Tony said she thought we were an *experiment* – God was bored and just created us for amusement, a sort of cosmic joke and curious, perhaps, of the outcome. *That's original*, I thought. Giving the creation myth your own peculiar twist – God being *bored*! I wonder whether God is still curious or has since lost interest now the joke's on us? Anyway, he can always wipe the slate clean and start afresh. Apocalypse now, please; we've had our chance!

The Danish philosopher, Søren Kierkegaard, also took up on the idea of boredom but extended it to the whole of mankind:

'The gods were bored, so they created man. Adam was bored because he was alone, so Eve was created, [...] then Adam and Eve and Cain and Abel were bored *en famille*, then [...] the people were bored *en masse*. To divert themselves, they conceived the idea of constructing a tower high enough to reach the heavens. This idea itself is as boring as the tower was high, and constitutes a terrible proof of how boredom has gained the upper hand'.[40]

Boredom aside, note that Kierkegaard here departs from the idea of a *single* creator. He says the '*gods* were bored'. As a

---

40   Søren Kierkegaard, *Either/Or* (cited in Colin Wilson, *The Outsider*, 259).

modern thinker, he will have nothing to do with the belief that has been predominant for over 4000 years: the *biblical* myth of creation.

Taken literally, this myth does answer all the questions. Of *origin*: we were created by God; of *nature*: we are placed somewhere between the beasts and the angels; and of *purpose*: to multiply, replenish and subdue the earth. Problem solved! No wonder this narrative has been adopted by the major religions, Judaism, Christianity and Islam. In their obsessive attempt at mass conversion, they organised themselves around the concept of a *single* deity. 'Mohammed knew that monotheism was inimical to tribalism: a single deity who was the focus of all worship would integrate society as well as the individual'.[41] Historically then, monotheism became mainstream at the cost of other myths or beliefs. The latter have since fallen off the radar. Collateral damage as it were. Now, there's something to complain about! Yet despite this dominance, we may still take a closer look at the questions of origin, nature and purpose. OK, this myth was not meant to be taken literally, but we can still reflect on how far we have come in solving the puzzle.

According to the major religions, we were *created* in 'the image of God'. According to science, we have *evolved* from apes. Ever since the publication of Charles Darwin's *Origin of the Species* in 1859, an 'evolutionary' theory has been presented as an alternative to the idea of a God creator.

Brought up in the Catholic faith but also as a free spirit, Tony found this idea ridiculous. "Evolved from apes my foot, then why haven't they found the 'missing link' yet?" she retorted. "Why, because it's simply not there!"

To be honest, I agreed with her on this, even though I didn't share her faith. Evolution, nope, don't buy it! Creation at least has an aura of credibility, a spiritual dimension of unfathomable

---

41   Karen Armstrong, *A History of God*, 175.

scrutiny. A blow in the face of rational thinking man. That alone gets my vote!

So, the evolutionists, wishing a more 'rational' explanation of the origin of existence, simply inverted the equation – it was not God that created man, but man that created God! Thus, the traditional interpretation was now open to revision! This is the starting point Karen Armstrong takes in her illuminating study *A History of God*. The book opens with the sentence, 'In the beginning, *human beings created a God* who was the First Cause of all things and Ruler of heaven and earth'. This, she continues, is 'one of the earliest ideas *evolved by human beings* to explain the mystery and tragedy of life'[42] [italics added], further implying that 'God alone had reality and only he could redeem us from nothingness'.[43] Yet as time elapsed, the reality of this One God proved so 'remote', so 'rationally incomprehensible', that he seems to have 'passed out of our consciousness'.

For contemporary man, this blueprint has indeed lost its sex-appeal. After such a long innings, its answers are no longer historically accepted. Atheism, which Armstrong describes as 'an automatic response to the experience of living in a secularised society', is now the 'prevailing mood'.[44] Hence, not long after Darwin's death blow, one atheistic Western philosopher could cry out, 'Where is God? We have killed him'.[45]

If man's origin is debatable, what then of his *nature*, a creature somewhere between the beasts and the angels. 'Somewhere between', what exactly does that mean? This is where the fun begins, for here we really are in the dark. Many have toyed with this question and imaginations have run riot. Mine included. In

---

42   Ibid, 9–10; here Armstrong is paraphrasing Wilhelm Schmidt's *The Origin of the Idea of God* (1912).
43   Ibid, 195.
44   Ibid, 433.
45   Friedrich Nietzsche, *The Gay Science* (1st publ. 1882, New York, 1974), No. 125.

fact, I find it impossible to look at people without comparing them to some sort of beast – animal, bird, fish, insect or reptile – either in appearance or behaviour, or both. This passage by D.H. Lawrence, must surely feel familiar:

'She too was fascinated by him, fascinated, as if some strange creature, a rabbit or a bat, or a brown seal, had begun to talk to her'.[46]

In my horoscope, I am *Aries* the ram, derivation of my family name, *Ayress* (*nomen est omen*!). But in the Chinese calendar, I fall under the year of the ape (hence my fear of the idea of evolution!). Actually, I do have something of both the ram and ape, though I feel closer to the panther, and Tony, to confuse matters further, saw me as a deer due to my graceful, light-footed way of walking! Well, I guess there's something in that too, though I'm still struggling with the antlers!

For many evolutionists and other megalomaniacs who like to play for God, 'somewhere between' means somewhere *towards*. Not happy with simply occupying the 'middle station', they argue that we are in the process of evolving from a bestial past to a God-like future. In *Thus Spoke Zarathustra*, Nietzsche sees man as a 'tightrope' stretched over the abyss between the 'Ape and the Superman'. Man is not an end in itself but a being to be overcome. But to cross this bridge, he must become a 'tightrope walker'. A heady philosophy, not for the faint-hearted! And Freud too, peering into the unconscious depths of his patients, sees only the 'old *reptilian* brain', preventing progression towards a more rational and civilised state.

The notion that we are somehow 'unfinished', a passing stage yet to be overcome, does have traction, but to what end exactly? Luckily, creatures do seem to be an insistent part of our make-up. Without them, we may end up as robots or some form of artificial intelligence. Heaven forbid! Not as angels, of course;

---

46   *Women in Love*, 480.

they're off the radar, too. Is our nature then, still a book waiting to be written?

And finally, what of our *purpose* – multiply, replenish and subdue the earth. As far as the first goes, mission accomplished – we fornicate like rabbits (oops, sorry, another comparison) and there are now *billions* of us banging on in perpetuity; as for replenishing the earth, well, mission accomplished, too. Our industrious nature has replenished the planet to repletion, only to wallow in its excess and *pollute* like self-satisfied humans; and thirdly, to subdue or 'have dominion over every living thing'. Here too, we have been rather overzealous with the brief, reinterpreting it along the way from having 'dominion' over all, to *destroying* all. To paraphrase Yuval Noah Harari, Homo sapiens have climbed to the top rung in the food chain, becoming the deadliest species in the annals of planet Earth. With the added 'dubious distinction' of having a track record like an 'ecological serial killer', altogether a 'terrestrial menace'.[47] Our purpose, it would seem, has run its course!

We have come full circle. Arguably, there *are* a great number of ailing plants, and their outlook on life *is* bleak. This is attested by a long-standing legacy of intellectual endeavour. It is tempting to brush this aside as a 'self-fulfilling prophecy'. I am sick, *ergo*, the world is sick. Yet the reverse is also true – the world is sick, *ergo*, I am sick. Both are interrelated as two sides of a coin. We cannot deny that for the ailing plant, it is difficult to see the world in a positive light. But his 'sickness' is related to the world he lives in. It shapes his view as much as he wishes to perceive.

If he does get to see paradise at all, it is invariably a glimpse, a fleeting moment of bliss. Even a notoriously pessimistic novelist as Graham Greene could find solace in the autumn season in his hometown, Antibes. In his novel, *May We Borrow Your Husband?*, he describes the feeling when all the holiday crowds had left:

---

47 *Sapiens*, 70–82.

'For a man who has reached the age when all he wants is some good wine and some good cheese and a little work, it is the best season of all'.[48]

Nikos Kazantzakis, author of *Zorba the Greek*, which became a major film, was asked to summarise the message of the film. His answer is a classic expression of a glimpse of bliss on earth:

'How simple and frugal a thing is happiness: a glass of wine, a roast chestnut, a wretched little brazier, and the sound of the sea'.[49]

Apart from the 'wretched little brazier', which involves toil to keep it going, this description also includes an essential ingredient: *wine*! The intoxication brought about by alcohol dulls the jarring reality of everyday existence. No more cares, no more worries. 'The drunken consciousness', says William James, 'is one bit of the mystic consciousness. […] Sobriety diminishes, discriminates, and says no; drunkenness expands, unites, and says yes. It is in fact the great exciter of the *Yes* function in man […] It makes him for the moment one with truth'.[50]

It is interesting to reflect that while 'the good Christian' has 'a lifetime to drink wine', 'the good Muslim' has 'an eternity'. Where Christianity has no qualms about 'terrestrial drinking', the Koran distinctly frowns upon it, seeing it as 'simultaneously evil and paradisiacal'. Only in paradise are the righteous promised 'rivers of wine delicious to those who drink…'[51] Presumably, once in paradise, the 'evil' influence of wine is distilled, leaving only its heavenly after-effect!

For ailing plants searching for paradise and crying out for help, alcohol or a narcotic drug, offers a quick solution, albeit

---

48 Quoted in Ted Jones, *The French Riviera* (London, 2007), 64.
49 Ibid, 61.
50 *The Varieties of Religious Experience*, 304–305.
51 Mark Forsyth, *A Short History of Drunkenness* (London, 2018), 104–106.

temporary. A proven panacea that helps them escape the painful reality of *Weltschmerz*. It is one way of coping with life while struggling with its meaning. For the puzzle still remains: his origin is debatable, his nature unclear, and his purpose to be reviewed. To this, the *healthy* plants raise their glasses and sing out, 'Always Look on the Bright Side of Life'.[52] How easy for them, they were born in paradise!

---

52 A song title from the film, *Monty Python's Life of Brian* (1979).

'Shall I compare thee to a Summer day?'

William Shakespeare, Sonnet 18

Chapter Five
A Rose, a Sweet, Sweet Rose

Not wishing the pessimists to have the day, we must move on. We still need to find answers to the bugging questions: How should we then live and in what direction do we go? We have reflected on the importance of establishing a firm footing in life. From the first three years, to childhood, and on through adolescence into adulthood. And yes, our origins *are* debatable, so what? Our nature *is* unclear, who gives a monkey's (comparison intended!)? Our purpose *is* spent. Now, there's a challenge! Upbringing is our only chance, and we have, at best, twenty years to get it right.

If we don't get off to a good start – happy mum, happy baby – what are our chances of survival? With an expectant high casualty rate and risk of permanently damaged goods, the general consensus is not optimistic. If we are lucky to escape a pathological career, the chances are that we will only have the blight of *Weltschmerz* to contend with! This is where the struggle for meaning and purpose starts. And this is where *healthy* plants can lend a hand. Without them, we're on our own.

Tony was sixteen years young – sweet sixteen – when World War II broke out and a young woman of twenty-one when it ended. This coincided precisely with the period in a young girl's life when love and romance is in the air, when life blossoms with vibrant expectation and personality begins to take form. Tears begin to flow as I write this, romantic fool that I am. And now, of all times, Holland was overrun by German forces and normal life took on the grim reality of wartime. I can hear the pessimist saying, 'well, there goes her youth down the drain'. But no, the very opposite is true!

Browsing through her wartime diaries (1939–1945), one cannot escape the impression that here is a teenage girl straining at the leash. War, what war? Her diaries are crammed full of entries of family visits, shopping sprees, music, film and theatre, adventures with friends and, of course, flirtations with budding suitors. As if all was business as usual. In one entry she records, with the nonchalance of youth, how she dealt with one very persistent admirer. On arriving home after a day out somewhere, she finds the boy in question waiting for her.

"I think this chap is in love with you, judging from his letters," says her mother.

"Well, I haven't answered any," Tony replies.

"The last one I sent you was rather nice," the boy cuts in.

"Yes, but it had three spelling mistakes!" was Tony's devastating reply, and the entry concludes with how chagrined the young man looked. The victorious smile on her face is almost visible!

Other entries bear witness to countless trips to various towns, shopping, going to the theatre or staying overnight with friends. She was never alone; there was always somewhere to go or someone to have fun with. Especially her favourite cousin, whom I shall call Mary. They had a lot of fun together and shared many experiences. In one entry, she describes how they could hardly walk from laughing, dragging their heavy cases along and ending up collapsing in the snow, still giggling! Speaking of which, throwing snowballs seems to have been their favourite distraction. At people, cars, windows or whatever took their fancy. 'Scandalous behaviour, really', she writes, 'but such fun!' After one long period of snow, a thaw set in, and her entry reads, 'Thaw, bah!' This exclamation crops up regularly. Just as regular as the exclamation 'Goh', which we discussed earlier. These were her favourites, and she used them throughout her whole life. Another word she often used was 'dull'. If there was nothing special happening or nowhere to go, the entry would simply read, 'dull'. Not bored in the sense of *ennui*, she was never bored in that way, but bored in the sense of uneventful. She was too full of life; she wanted to make things happen. War, or no war.

Parties and dancing, too, there were plenty of those. It was at one of these, in 1943, that she first met her future husband. In an entry, we learn that he enquired of the group then present, who the pretty girl was that had stayed at so-and-so's place (he probably already knew but was fishing for an introduction). They nodded towards Tony who denied this, saying that it was someone else. She was accustomed to many suitors and played hard to get. She could afford to be choosy and didn't want to rush and regret making the wrong choice. In a later entry, she admits finding his attention 'nice'.

Yet it wasn't all just fun and play. In between the romancing, her personality was developing, and she was inquisitive and eager to learn. Whatever the subject, she took every available opportunity. In music and theatre, we find her writing down her experiences. And even after the war too, we find many entries in her post-war diaries (1946–1949) of popular American songs at the time. A particular favourite was the song 'With a Song in My Heart'. She was fond of classical music, too, and wrote down many melodies, using a number system for the intervals between the notes. Thus, we may find the name of a piece with its accompanying string of digits – 5 1 2 3 4 5 5 5 6 6 6 5 – or a string of digits followed by the query, 'what's the name of this piece?' Or a play at a theatre she had just seen. She wrote down the gist of the scenes and the names of the characters. Do you know anyone who would do this? Most of us would make do with the programme and perhaps keep it as a souvenir. And these entries are not just one-off; they occur all the time. As if she were trying to capture the experience and commit it to memory. To make it a lasting impression. It was her way of learning what life had to offer and was always intense and personal.

The first entry to her diary of 1942 reads like a New Year's resolution. Translated, which does it no justice, we read: 'true love exists in the neglect of one's own ego'. Is this still our fun-loving girl? And an entry discussing the great cathedrals of Europe. Describing Chartres, she quotes Napoleon, who is reputed to have said, 'one enters this magnificent structure as an atheist, and emerges as a believer'! Further, there are comments on books she has recently read and book titles she intends to read. And hardly a page can be turned without an illustration, cartoon or detailed drawing. What we see here is a *Fräulein*, enthralled with the world and quivering with excitement in absorbing it all. Wonderful!

If this isn't a description of a healthy plant, then I don't know what is. And if this is all due to love and attention during childhood, then what more is there to be said? I rest my case. Yet though the firm footing has been established, purpose and meaning have not. The war is now over and a future beckons. Marriage, and a career maybe, loom on the horizon. Tony still needs to find direction and purpose in her life. But first, I must recount the incident of the near-fatal bullet.

Tony was born in Heino, a small rural town situated in the north-eastern province of Overijssel. Her father was the local notary, and because the house was large and in a central location, it was billeted by German officers. Her father's office and all its documents had to be removed to make way for the new occupants. Thus, she and her parents moved upstairs but were still allowed to use the kitchen, which was always stocked with provisions, even during the period of food rationing.

At the end of the war, during the liberation, the German troops gradually pulled back and often left snipers behind to cover their retreat. So too, in Heino. The troops began to pull out, and one by one, the inhabitants cautiously emerged from their shelters. No one realised that a German sniper was still up in the church tower. Tony's father wanted to reinstall his office as soon as possible. So, they – Tony, her parents and the housemaid – all started throwing boxes out of the upstairs window. Presumably, this was easier than lugging everything down via the stairs. The sniper, viewing all this activity from his vantage point, became increasingly nervous or irritated. With heads constantly popping in and out of the window he was unable to restrain himself, aimed and fired a shot...

Tony told me that she remembered hearing a sort of 'whooshing' noise that sounded very close but didn't know what it was. It was only the next morning, after hearing the maid cry out, that they discovered a five-inch bullet embedded in the window frame, exactly where they had been popping their heads out! It must have passed within millimetres of Tony's head, but miraculously, she was not hit. She lived to tell the tale. I still have the bullet case as proof and the reminder that, without her guardian angel, I would never have met her and not be writing her story now. How I love fate!

So, she emerges from the war intact, with a *fiancé* and a life ahead of her. And now she seems to waver between a number of possibilities, as if trying to feel where her growing personality is leading her. The chance of a scholarship in archaeology at the British Museum has just been dashed by her father's disapproval, mentioned in the first chapter.

Now, there is this new American film industry which, in the aftermath of the war, is rapidly gaining popularity in Europe.

Aware of her good looks, she toys with the idea of becoming a model or film actress. She has a collection of picture postcards of all the film stars of the day: Gary Grant, Deanna Durbin, James Stuart, Zarah Leander, Errol Flynn, Joan Crawford and many others. It is a world that fascinates her, and especially Deanna Durbin, who seems to have been a bit of a role model. She has many photos of her and sees a likeness, both in looks and temperament. Looks is one thing, but she doubts her acting ability. Perhaps not quite her thing?

Marriage then? A wedding date is set: 22nd August 1946.

On the day before the wedding, her mother finds her looking wistfully out of the window. "Are you having any doubts, my child?"

"Oh, Mama," she replies, "am I doing the right thing?"

"You still love him, don't you?" her mother asks.

"I guess so," Tony replies, a little hesitantly. "Anyway, he's very clever, so at least I'll have intelligent children!" She is staring into the future, trying to visualise or anticipate what married life has in store for her. She makes her choice, says farewell to the glamour and gets married!

Her husband, well aware of the prize catch he has made, is not reluctant to show her off to the world. Travels through Europe follow – Italy, Switzerland, France and Germany – and children, too. Four in total, and she is devoted to them all. As we noted earlier, there are two types of women: those devoted to the husband, and those devoted to the children. The latter rarely divorce, at least not while the children are still young. The psychology here I leave you to work out!

Though resigned to marriage and the upbringing of her children, the world of glamour still haunts and tempts her. In her diary of 1949, there is an entry in the form of a draft letter of her intention to write to a film producer (whose name is not mentioned). She says when going to the pictures, she can't help but notice that 'the crowd always love a *girl meets boy* film'. She and her husband love his films and wonder if he would be interested in the following scenario. It is based on a recent trip to Rome with her favourite cousin, Mary, where both girls experienced the amorous advances of Italian would-be lovers. Tony then describes the opening scene: 'a group of young girls embark on a train for a holiday to Rome. This must be accompanied with appropriate music, talk of Italian decorum and joking among the girls…'. Here, the entry abruptly stops and presumably didn't get any further than this initial draft. Was she still thinking, if not a film actress, then perhaps a scriptwriter?

And what about modelling? Yes, she does follow up on that. With trips to a studio in Amsterdam, and numerous photo sessions where she poses in a wide variety of outfits, ranging from bathing costumes to evening gowns. Even before this period, photos show her posing elegantly and fully aware of how to look into a camera for optimal effect, and yes, photogenic, too. I believe all this started at quite an early age, when her parents, obviously proud of their daughter, had many photos taken professionally of her. Poise and elegance came naturally, and she carried these throughout her whole life. 'Call me Madam!' was a phrase she invariably used when demanding respect, as the situation required. Even in her final phase of Alzheimer's, her carers used to remark with surprise, how elegant she wished to remain, with her clothes correctly adjusted!

But even more important than her clothes was her hair. Everybody remarked on how beautiful it was. That was her showstopper. She went to great lengths finding hairdressers who did her hair as *she* wanted.

"They don't listen," she would complain. "They keep wanting to try out their own ideas, how awful they can be!"

When she did find the right one, she was over the moon – if her hair looked good, she felt good! The very last trip her children and I made with her, getting her outside in the wheelchair, was to her hairdresser. Though she hardly spoke anymore, the enjoyment she got from this visit was clear for all to see. She was ready again to face the world!

Yes, she was a lady to be reckoned with. She knew her place and knew what she wanted. And at the same time modest, kind and loving. With the looks of a diva but not the attitude. With the air of a woman of the world, but with the spontaneity and outlook of a child. With a love of learning almost scholarly, and the eye of an artist. All these qualities combined in one woman, quite remarkable! The war, if it did have any effect on her, compounded her ability of distinguishing between the good, the bad and the ugly. She saw straight into the heart of things, which helped her find purpose and direction. Who to approach, and who to avoid. Which undertaking was worth pursuing and which was not. In one sense, her world was black and white. People were either good or bad, nice or rotten. Artefacts were either artistic and useful, or ugly and worthless! The grey area in between, which for most of us is quite large, was for her small and less relevant. Though she was not blind to this reality, and always willing to help a struggling soul, a clear choice did help her find direction and purpose in life.

So that's it then is it, that's what we need, a clear choice? Yes, Tony would say. You must develop your talents and have faith in their outcome. And always, always try to distinguish between the good, the bad and the ugly. Make use of your talents and observe people for what they really are. This was a major part of her philosophy that she tried to impart on her children and also imparted on me.

Her eldest son, whom I shall call Raymond, had a singular talent in mathematics and was a whizz kid at school. At an early age, his grandpa once gave him a self-made gadget, comprising a lamp, battery and switch. Flip the switch and on went the lamp. Switch it back again and off went the lamp. Raymond was fascinated. On, off, on, off, click, click, click… at bedtime they still heard him clicking and saying, "On, off, on, off,", until he clicked himself to sleep! Later, his father saw a career for him as an engineer in the multinational company where he worked. Raymond however, thought otherwise. An engineer, sure, but following in his father's footsteps in the multinational, no way! Tony helped him free himself from his father's pressure. Using her contacts in the USA, she paved the way for his entrance to a prestigious university in California, where he graduated in atomic physics. Though it broke her heart to see him leave, she knew what it meant to have the opportunity to follow one's talents. Being her first baby, their bond was very close, and it was his welfare that she had at heart. On her deathbed, it was the knowledge of his hasty return from the States that kept her alive. Upon arrival, he rushed to her apartment and embraced her for the last time. Fifteen minutes later, she passed away. What a lovely end.

Her daughter, whom I shall call Emily, inherited her mother's artistic talents but also a passion for flying from her father's side. She made a career with the national airline and took to flying her own Piper-Cup sport plane. But she never lost her interest in art, especially sculpting, which she still does today. She often asked her mother and was puzzled why she didn't paint more and exhibit her works.

"Because I'm not that sort of a painter," her mother replied. "I paint purely for personal satisfaction."

Emily later took it upon herself to bind many of her mother's drawings and pictures into an album. Her mother loved it when she visited her, and they would sit and browse through the book together. That was a great joy. Making use of your talents does not necessarily mean exploiting them *all*. This, of course, is only true for multi-talented people. I think Emily understood this.

Her second son and third in line, whom I shall call Harry, inherited her inquisitive nature and love of life. He was a good-looking child and was much pampered by everyone. Tony, afraid that this would upset the balance, tried to counteract all this attention, but this was like fighting the wind. Thus, despite her efforts, Harry received much love and attention, thereby guaranteeing his firm footing! He was most interested in mechanics, how things worked. As a baby, he once received a toy figure that was weighted down with a heavy substance. He shook it to and fro and uttered the magic word: "Sand!"

"Aha," cried his grandpa, "that's gonna be another engineer in the family!"

Like his mother, Harry was a self-possessed child who knew what he wanted and wanted to know everything. He studied mechanical engineering and started his own software company. Passionate about how things worked and wanting to make things happen. He oozed self-confidence, which is not surprising, given the mother he had!

On one occasion, when he was nearing the age of getting his driving licence, his mother took him in the car to the nearby market square. It was covered in snow, and as nobody was around, she said, "Now it's time for you to learn how to skid with the car!" She showed him how it was done and then let him try. At that moment, a police car pulled up and the officer asked what was going on. "I'm teaching my son how to skid," replied Tony.

"Yes, I can see that," said the officer. "But it's not allowed and dangerous here in a public place."

"Well, there's nobody about," Tony answered. "And I would rather teach him myself than have him trying it alone."

The officer saw the sense of this argument, noted her smile and let them off with a warning. Fantastic! How many mothers do you know who operate like that? That's the way to bring up kids.

Her youngest son, whom I shall call Ron, was an adorable child with a kind, loving nature. He looked up to Harry and, to a certain degree, lived in his shadow. Whenever someone called on the phone, he would answer in a timid voice, "It's *just* Ron speaking." Yet what he lacked in self-confidence, he made up with kindness. He was much-loved and made friends easily. He had a caring personality and would have made an excellent doctor. I say *would* have, if fate had chosen otherwise. Due to the large number of aspirant medical students, candidates were selected by drawing lots. Ron's lot, alas, was not drawn. Everyone was disappointed, Tony foremost. She urged him to try elsewhere, even abroad, but he didn't want to leave his friends and neighbourhood. Such a pity, he would indeed have made a great doctor, as caring for others was his second nature. *C'est la vie!*

Of all her children, Ron was the closest. He visited her regularly and even joined us on holidays together. Tony often took the opportunity, on these occasions, to work on his self-confidence and lack of patience. We would agree to meet at some cafe at a certain time, and it was always Ron who was there first but just hanging around instead of sitting at a table with a drink.

"Hello, dear Ron," she would call as soon as she saw him. "Didn't you manage to find a table?"

"No, I waited for you to arrive first," he replied.

"Oh, you sweet little boy, always thinking of others first!"

And then there was the car parking. If there was no space available, Ron would just loose his patience. He invariably drove straight off and parked 'just nearby', as he called it. We knew, however, what that meant: that he had parked a good ten-minute walk away! When he arrived a little hot and flustered, we would be sitting in the shade with a cool drink.

"Where are you parked?" he asked.

"Right there," we said, pointing to our car just a few spaces away.

He knew what would follow. When we arrive, we calmly assess the situation. Tony looks to the right and I to the left. Not so much for a vacant space but to the people around. Is there anybody approaching with a key in their hand? Is there anybody in a car about to drive away, or let's just drive around for a bit; someone's sure to leave soon. This strategy rarely failed. But try as we did to impress this on Ron, he just couldn't take this advice on board.

Sometimes, his mother would say, "You have to look further than your nose is long. Observe the surroundings and the people in it before you make a decision." I guess this advice is just not suited to everybody.

If there is one episode that characterises Tony best of all, it must be the incident of the missing corkscrew. It occurred during a holiday in France. The whole family was together, and we hired a boat for the day. One of those old-fashioned river boats you might see in impressionist paintings: long, narrow, with high, open sides and a canopy top. Not the punting variety, though, but equipped with a foul-smelling motor engine.

Everyone was on board and, most importantly, lunch was packed: pâté, cheese, French bread, fruit, wine and water. Off we went, cruising peacefully along and looking for a nice spot to have our picnic. We found a lovely sunny glade next to an overhanging willow tree and moored the boat. Out came the lunch, bread, cheese and pâté. Bottles of wine and glasses were placed on the table. Who was going to open the wine? Where was the corkscrew? What do you mean it's not there? No corkscrew! That's when the panic started.

With accusations, "How could you forget the corkscrew?", "Why didn't you check if we had it?", "Does anyone have a corkscrew?"; with frantic searching, seats were lifted, doors were opened, the boat was ransacked, while others ransacked their brains for alternative ways of opening a bottle of wine. All to no avail.

And then, just before a drastic measure was taken, Tony spoke up. "Wait," she cried. "What's that up there?" She was pointing to something metal sticking out of a wooden beam under the canopy. On inspection, it proved to be, *Mon Dieu!* – a corkscrew! Of course, a French boat without a corkscrew, unthinkable. *Why didn't we think of that?*

"Mother, you're a genius," they all called.

"Well," she replied in her usual, calm way, "we are in *France* after all."

Like a Hercule Poirot mystery, the solution often stares you in the face, only you can't see it. While we all looked down and around, Tony was the only one who looked *up* towards the canopy. We were searching but not *looking*; we were too busy trying to figure out how to open a bottle *without* a corkscrew. But she knew there *must* be a corkscrew somewhere. In our turmoil, we lost our focus. Tony was the only one who was still *really* in France. She saw it because she knew where she was, trusted her intuition and cast her artist's eye over the scene. During the frenzy, she remained serene and observant as ever.

This is such a wonderful story. How Tony, in her quiet, unassuming manner, put a boatload of intellect to shame. A definitive Zen moment for the record. Amazing what a sweet rose can do!

> *'So we beat on, boats against the current,
> borne back ceaselessly into the past.'*
>
> F. Scott Fitzgerald, The Great Gatsby

Chapter Six

Forward to the Past

In the Great Chain of Being then, where do we stand? Our *nature* – somewhere between the beasts and angels – is vague and unfixed. Does this admit metamorphosis, collectively or individually, for some of us seem more like animals while others more like angels? And, among men, are we a rose on the dunghill or a fool on the hill, or just one of the crowd? Tony believed that *whoever* we are, it is important to put our talents to good use. Our talents, and how we use them, defines our *purpose* in life. A purpose, in the beginning, to 'multiply, replenish and dominate', which required of us ethical actions to promote survival and well-being. The ethical or moral aspects are still there, as is the need for clear choices, one way or the other. Without a definite stand, we are but driftwood, adrift at sea with no purpose or meaning. Let us further reflect on some existing ideas on the nature and purpose of our existence, again with Tony as support.

In 'man's continuing quest to understand his world', we are, says Daniel Boorstin:

'Caught between two eternities – the vanished past and the unknown future – we never cease to seek our bearings and our sense of direction…'[53]

The idea of being 'caught' between the past and future is both arresting and suggestive, but to state that the past has 'vanished' and the future 'unknown' blurs the boundaries so that we are not only caught but stranded as well! To believe that we cannot go back, for there is nothing to go back to, is deceptive. The past has neither vanished nor would we want it to. The fool on the hill smiles, seeing what the crowd does not. He will neither dismiss the past nor share their blind foraging into the future and observes them rushing madly on like lemmings to the sea. We cannot escape the past, and the future is not entirely unknown, for we hold it in our hands. Granted, *time* does march on, but to what exactly? Perhaps we are just destined to mark time only!

According to Freud:

'The question of the purpose of human life has been raised countless times; it has never yet received a satisfactory answer and perhaps does not admit of one [...] only religion can answer the question of the purpose of life. [...] We will therefore turn to the less ambitious question of what men themselves show by their behaviour to be the purpose and intention of their lives. [...] The answer to this can hardly be in doubt. They strive after happiness'.[54]

Of the two aspects identified by Freud – religion and human happiness – only the latter, he says, is worthy of our attention. The former is too ambitious and must be dismissed:

'Religion [...] imposes equally on everyone its own path to the acquisition of happiness and protection from suffering. Its technique consists in depressing the value of life and distorting the picture of the real world in a delusional manner – which [...] by drawing them into a mass-delusion, religion succeeds in

---
53 *The Seekers*, xiii.
54 *Civilization and its Discontents*, 12–13.

sparing many people an individual neurosis. But hardly anything more'.[55]

Like Marx before him, Freud dismisses religion as nothing more than the 'opiate of the masses'. A drug that diverts mankind from the business at hand, i.e. the practical pursuit of happiness through the *scientific* study of human behaviour. For Marx, this was the field of economics, for Freud, psychoanalysis. As we are here but 'reflecting', it is beyond our scope to study their views in detail. Suffice it to say that both thinkers agree on the following: religion is rejected as self-delusional; if paradise exists, it is to be found here, on earth; and its attainability is not dependent on providence but on human intervention, within a historical process. They emphasise faith in man's rational ability to shape his universe and belief in evolutionary progress. Altogether, an unmistakable expression of the prevalent mood of atheism. No wonder such 'worldly' philosophers have proved so influential in mainstream modern thought. But *mainstream* thought is not the whole picture. And for that very reason, they got some of it wrong!

As the reader by now will be aware, we do not view the future in terms of evolutionary progress. Not as fittingly described by the Marxist philosopher, Ernst Bloch (1884–1977):

'The whole of human life was directed towards the future: we experience our lives as incomplete and unfinished. Unlike animals, we are never satisfied but always want more'.[56]

How, Tony would say, can we be directed towards the future if we have yet to understand the past! And if we are 'incomplete and unfinished', then it is the past that has made us so. No, if we *are* directed towards the future, it is because we have turned our back on the past, wishing to *escape* it. No, the whole idea of progress is just too arrogant, too self-centred. Self-congratulatory

---

55 Ibid, 21–22.
56 Cited in Karen Armstrong, *A History of God*, 445.

intoxication. Take the more contemplative French writer, Marcel Proust, for example. He looked at the question from quite a different angle:

'All that we can say is that everything is arranged in this life as though we entered it carrying a burden of obligations contracted in a former life [...] to do good, to be kind and thoughtful [...]. All these obligations [...] seem to belong to a different world [...] a world entirely different from this one and which we leave in order to be born on this earth, before perhaps returning there to live once again beneath the sway of those unknown laws which we obeyed because we bore their precepts in our hearts, *not knowing* whose hand had traced them there'.[57] [Italics added.]

If we know nothing for certain, then we cannot *know* where we are going, or even what we are. 'There are more things in heaven and earth, Horatio, than are dreamt of in your philosophy',[58] says Shakespeare, or, in the words of D.H. Lawrence, 'After all, what is mankind but just one expression of the incomprehensible'.[59] In the face of nothingness, and caught between the past and future, we are in need of some faith. Not just 'cautious' speculation, but some firm footing to establish our goings.

In his last novel *Resurrection*, Tolstoy describes the views of the peasant Nabatov on religion and the social upheaval caused by the Revolution. For all it contains, the passage is worth quoting in full:

'The revolution, according to him, ought not to change the people's basic way of living [...], ought not to destroy the whole fabric but only alter the inner workings of the great, solid, beautiful old structure he loved so passionately.

He was also a typical peasant in his views on religion: he never thought about metaphysical problems, about the origin of all origins or life in the next world. To him, [...] God was

---

57 *Remembrance of Things Past*:3, 186.
58 W. Shakespeare, *Hamlet*, Act 1, Scene V.
59 *Women in Love*, 65.

a hypothesis for which, so far, he had had no use. He was not in the least concerned about the origin of the universe, and did not care whether Moses or Darwin were right, and Darwinism, which seemed so important to his associates, he took no more seriously than the story of the creation in six days.

He was not interested in the question of how the world came into being, just because he was constantly occupied by the question of *how best to live in this world*. Nor did he ever think of the *future life*, having inherited from his ancestors the firm and calm belief, common to all who till the soil, that just as in the animal and vegetable kingdoms nothing ceases to exist but is continually being transformed from one thing into another – manure into grain, grain into fowl, tadpole into frog, caterpillar into butterfly, acorn into oak – so man does not perish either but only undergoes a change. This he believed, and therefore he always looked death bravely and even gaily in the eye and unflinchingly bore the suffering that leads up to it; but he did not like and did not know how to talk about these things. He was fond of work and was always busy with practical affairs, and encouraged his comrades to do the same'.[60] [Italics added.]

I know Tony had read some of his work, but we never really discussed Tolstoy. Partly due to the fact that I only read him later on in life. A pity, because he has much to offer. The firm footing he here describes, the 'great, solid, beautiful old structure' of country life, is, for Tolstoy, a 'basic way of living'. For Marx however, this 'idiocy of rural life', as he called it, has been for centuries an obstacle to economic progress! It would appear that one man's meat is another man's poison.

Marx, and his mainstream followers, write Tolstoy off as a romantic dreamer, clinging to a way of life that is being replaced. Technical and economic progress, they say, involves necessary offers. On that score, they are right. Modern civilisation *is* too

---

60   *Resurrection*, 503–504.

complex to ride on a rural economy alone. But the strength of their argument rests chiefly on a tidal wave. An historical process, which, they argue, is just the 'natural' course of things. A road map of linear evolution, which the majority follow in their sleepwalk, like, we may jeeringly add, a 'one-eyed king leading the blind'!

Yet, to pass Tolstoy off as a 'romantic dreamer' weeping for a bygone age, is unfair. Granted, he was not mainstream, but neither was he blind. Indeed, he was as much a reformer as Marx, insofar he sought to reform the 'institutions of this globe', in particular, the criminal and penal code. But Tolstoy was not interested in the *economic* 'historical reality of the given moment'. His quest was on the 'ethical plane', his business was with the '*transcendental*'. On this, Rosemary Edmonds writes:

'Transfiguration, rather than revolution. It is impossible to establish justice on earth if people themselves do not suffer a sea-change and become 'different' by surmounting their narrow egoism, which is practicable only by considering meaning in relation to eternity, in contact with the Creator. But Tolstoy could never quite accept the fact that 'the law made nothing perfect' – that no law will turn bad people into good society. His hero does not see visions to send him winging his way to God: he must climb the laborious path of expiation, painful step after painful step, inspired only by an inner, 'moral' *desire* to atone'.[61]

Clearly, Marx and Tolstoy cannot agree on how best to live in this world. They differ both on focus (welfare or well-being), and on position (mainstream or sub-stream). Yet despite their differences, they both knew where they stood and applied their talents accordingly. Tolstoy, much later in life, after a personal crisis in his fifties; Marx, much earlier, from his days as a student of philosophy. They shared with us *their* views on the purpose of life. Where then, does that leave *us*? Arguably, these issues will

---

61 Rosemary Edmonds in her introduction to Tolstoy's *Resurrection*, 12–15.

divide us, likewise. We too, must navigate between ethical well-being and material welfare *and*, at the same time, recognise our position; do we jump on the bandwagon and go along with the crowd or pitch in with the 'party poopers' and spoil the fun?

On the *first* issue – the ethical and material motivation of our actions – Tony was quite clear. Basic material needs – food, clothing and shelter – underpin our welfare and are intrinsically good. Having enough money to spend, she said, does help, but doing the good or right thing is the chief aim in life. Beyond basic subsistence, money should only be used for that purpose. Doing the good or right thing was, for Tony, fundamental. Not something just to deliberate on or consider but an imperative for daily life. This means constantly choosing between good and evil. Between higher and baser motives.

Tony drew inspiration from the *Bible*. She spent at least an hour every day praying for others and reading her favourite passages. She dedicated many psalms to family and friends, writing their names at the head of the appointed psalm. Her bible was so worn with use that it was held together with paperclips and elastic bands! It was filled with notes and references to historical dates, names and events, where she tried to puzzle it all together. Whenever the subject of the *Bible* came up, it was always her eldest son, Raymond, who pointed out how much she knew about it. It was his indirect way of showing his admiration for her!

In much of what she wrote – prose, diary entries or loose notes – *Bible* quotes cropped up regularly. They were a major guide, helping her distinguish between the good, the bad, and the ugly. Though centuries old, the wisdom found in biblical parables and stories are just as relevant today. For many of us, who have been force-fed on the *Bible*, this is no longer palatable. We prefer to consume our wisdom based on a more contemporary diet and with topics we can relate to. But whether we read Tolstoy, telling us of people 'cheating and tormenting themselves', or a

Bible psalm, speaking of 'workers of iniquity' who 'eat up my people as they eat bread',[62] we cannot escape the exhortation not to leave off doing good.

To underline Tony's position, I would like to draw a parallel here with the English social critic and essayist, John Ruskin (1819–1900). In his famous attack on utilitarianism and the 'modern science' of political economy, he too, cited the *Bible* in stressing the importance of economic *justice*. It was this aspect, Ruskin argued, that the principal theorists – Adam Smith, John Stuart Mill and David Ricardo – had omitted in their definition of 'wealth'. He writes:

'... the final outcome and consummation of all wealth is in the producing as many as possible full-breathed, bright-eyed, and happy-hearted human creatures. Our modern wealth, I think, has rather a tendency the other way; – most political economists appearing to consider multitudes of human creatures not conducive to wealth, or at best conducive to it only by remaining in a dim-eyed and narrow-chested state of being'.[63]

Likewise, the utilitarian principal of 'the greatest happiness of the greatest number', which may sound politically correct but means nothing other, says Ruskin, than 'to be guided by balances of expediency', rather than by 'balances of justice'. Thus, he corrects, 'That country is the richest which nourishes the greatest number of *noble* and happy human beings.'[64] [Italics added.]

Tony also pointed out that God is often referred to in the *Bible* as being 'terrible' and 'jealous', quite the opposite of the merciful and loving picture painted by the Christian church. His 'wrath' and vengeful nature are well-documented. Not only is he the source of all good but also of all evil.

Speaking of which, Tony thought the scales were just tipped – fifty-one over forty-nine per cent – towards *evil*. That we therefore

---

62 Psalm XIV, 4 and LIII, 4.
63 *Unto This Last and Other Writings*, 189.
64 Ibid, page 169 and note 21.

find ourselves on a tilted plane that gravitates towards backsliding! Implying that the temptation to do bad pulls stronger than the prompting to do good. This concurs with Tolstoy's view of our needing to 'climb the laborious path of expiation', step by painful step. If it was the other way round, Tony argued, the incentive to do good would be too easy. We would be lulled into a false sense of well-being and relapse into a moral torpor. Whereas, to struggle against evil would give life meaning, a moral vigour to our existence. Giving in to evil confirms our baseness and corruptibility. Therefore, we must, and can, choose the path we take, easier for the healthy plant, challenging for the ailing one!

The *second* issue – mainstream or sub-stream – ostensibly involves *social* concerns, more than the material and ethical aspects of life; though, of course, they are all interrelated. And here, too, Tony knew where she stood. She stood her ground and refused to live according to the opinion of others; for that, Socrates somewhere says, is an 'illness'. Unlike me, who was too occupied with what others were doing and busy condemning the mob as stupid and blindly following each other. Tony never criticised others simply as conformists. Each according to his needs, she would say. Follow the truth and be true to yourself. She generally viewed the rebel or martyr with reservation, considering them more often foolish than wise, but held, at the same time, a certain admiration.

This was most noticeable in her reverence for the *Bible* prophets, particularly, Daniel and Isaiah. These were her 'heroes'. She loved to read of their fulminating against the ill-advised policies of the potentates and the idol-worshipping of the multitude. Even under threat of mortal punishment or death, they held firm to their insights and faith in the truth. Kings were often made to look foolish in the light of their prophecies, while the crowd cowered at the innate power they held. Jesus too, in his upturning of the 'money tables' and performing of miracles, would meet with Tony's approval! These were 'outsiders' that she understood and could relate to.

What she could not accept however, was their willingness to sacrifice their lives for their beliefs. This, in her view, was foolish.

"Life," she argued, "is a precious gift, a blessing and not to be traded in lightly."

"But isn't a *just* cause worth dying for?" I would reply.

"Better to lead others by example alive than to make your point dead," was her final answer, and the matter was closed!

The taking of life, by choice or otherwise, though understandable in a given situation, was for Tony a sacrilege. Suicide or martyrdom is a coward's way out! Life is worth *living* for, not surrendering or dying for. In fact, nothing in life is worth dying for – is it? The only concession to this rule, Tony once told me, was if someone tried to kill her father. She would not hesitate to kill the assailant with a potato knife (!) in her attempt to save him. For her children too, she would, if necessary, fight to the death. This is revealing, for it means, in Tony's mind, that *filial love* is the only cause worth dying for. To justify this view, I suppose we must assume that dying for one's beliefs or for one's loved ones are *not* the same thing. At least, not for Tony!

Though Tony was neither a fool on the hill, nor one of the crowd, she was, nevertheless, an outsider. Something I did not recognise at first. I thought that an outsider, per definition, stood 'outside' of society. A rebel, kicking *against* society, not moving along with it. Yet here was Tony, enjoying the crowd but immune to their stock responses; in the crowd, but impervious to their bleating and holding views as radical as any rebel.

"I'm not interested in *their* thoughts," she once said. "Mine are much more interesting!" If being self-possessed is an essential quality for an outsider, then she was qualified.

Brought up as a devout Catholic, was she never in conflict with the church? Yes, but she had no intention of joining those who would reform it. She remained a regular churchgoer, i.e.

went to pray and take communion. Later, as a divorcee and partner to a younger man, she knew there would be those who would frown upon her. Yet, that did not deter her from attending mass service and receiving the pastor's blessing. She even became a lector and was quite popular in the church community. But if she did not agree with the lesson she was given to read, she made her criticism plain to the pastor, hoping to win him over! It generally concerned a passage from the *Bible* that she was not impressed with, or it was just too contemporary for her liking. If she did not get her way, she sometimes took the liberty, during the reading, of emphasising the text where she thought it should be emphasised.

"They can't do anything about that," she remarked. "Besides, only the pastor would notice it." *Fait accompli,* as the French would say!

With the sermons too, she was equally outspoken. "David," she would say, 'I fell asleep during your sermon; it was rather boring. Where are the good old-fashioned sermons, with thunder and drama, to give us something to think about?" And when giving a compliment, it rarely lacked an element of mockery. "Nice sermon today, David; you spoke well. Not bad for a Protestant!" She often teased the pastor about his arrant protestant views, for she knew how he enjoyed these bouts of religious provocation. There were very few among the congregation who could test him at that level.

The point here is that Tony was, to the untrained eye, an ordinary Catholic churchgoer. She went to mass, prayed, took communion, and fulfilled her role as lector with dedication. But she also followed her own path, careful not to rock the boat too much. At her funeral service, pastor David alluded to this 'duality' by humorously reminding us how important it was to her that she looked the part and did the right things as lector. "Is my skirt straight?" and "Where would you like me to stand?" And, at the same time, from behind this pleasant exterior, she was intent on reading *her* version of the appointed text! Any attempt she made at 'reforming the system' was purely on a personal level. You can't change the world, she would say, but perhaps you *can* influence a few.

Mainstream or sub-stream. Before I met Tony, this was a clear-cut distinction. It still is, only now I see a greater range of variations. Yes, there is a herd instinct – the herd goes where the herd is led. I guess that's one definition of mainstream. And when a common practice becomes firmly established, it ends up as the 'establishment', and how delightful it is to kick against it! Especially when the system is blatantly wrong, and a rebellion is required to correct it. My good friend Brian would qualify as just such a rebel.

I think it all started after his 'state of the art' presentation, during a job interview. To showcase his ability in club repairing, Brian proudly presented two identical wooden club heads, displayed in a decorative wooden frame. One *before* renovation – worn and tattered – the other *after* renovation – gleaming, as if new. A formidable example of his craftsmanship. But to his great disappointment, it was met with the words, "What's this, a present?"

Brian returned from this affront, deflated. He just shook his head and repeated the famous words, "Pearls for the swine! Narrow-minded, complacent, and they've got the golf swing all wrong, too," he raged. I'm convinced that this singular episode, more than any other, hardened Brian's resolve to reform the golf establishment, in particular, the way golf was taught.

Perhaps 'reform' is not the right term. Though he may have initially hoped the golfing elite would see the error of their ways and adjust their position, Brian soon realised that developing his *own* method was the better option. Turn your back on the bandwagon and go your own way. He put all his teaching experience and accumulated insights on the golf swing into a book and went public. To date, his method – the *easiest* swing in golf – is gaining both adherents and in popularity. What once started as sub-stream may even end up mainstream – good on you, Brian!

Brian is an example of a rebel *with* a cause. He wanted to lead the golfing community away from the mainstream method of teaching golf, which, in his view, was *disabling* rather than empowering golfers in finding their potential and enjoying the game. Based on the free-flowing swings and mindset of such great golfers as Bobby and Ernest Jones, Brian developed a philosophy enabling an easy swing and a positive attitude. Since that great era back in the 1930s, golf, unfortunately, had taken a turn for the worse, becoming rigid and bogged down in mechanical thinking. This became common practice and was even promoted as progress!

Eighty years on, Brian had the courage to stick his neck out and shout, "Enough!" He side-stepped the establishment and, addressing the golfing community at large, pointed to the past, showing how they at least *understood* golf, providing future generations with a proven benchmark. A great example of moving forward to the past!

So, mainstream is not always synonymous with progress, and sub-stream can, in turn, become mainstream. Like, for example, Levi's jeans. A statement of rebellion when introduced in the 1950s, now mainstream and worn by all. Well, almost all. One day, a rebel will hopefully shout, "Enough," and refuse to wear them. Only then, will the herd instinct realise that it has followed one of the ugliest fashions for years! Functional, yes, complimentary, no.

And there are rebels, too, *without* a cause, who just kick out of resentment, uncertain where to direct their discontent, and establishments that have become so entrenched and pernicious that nothing but a revolution will undo them. The reader will appreciate that the terms mainstream and sub-stream are loose-fitting garments, designed for the purpose of clothing the argument. In general, mainstream may be taken to imply the existence of, or working of, a herd instinct, whereas sub-stream generally indicates its opposite. In that latter sense, the terms 'undertow', or 'counter-flow' might equally fit the bill.

It was only later, after fully understanding Tony's outsider position, that I was able to reassess the dynamics involved. Initially, I thought the mechanism was simple: mainstream contra sub-stream, i.e. sub-stream was right; mainstream was wrong! And there was every good reason for this. The herd is blind, stupid, easily hood-winked and led on, a fact well-attested. Whereas those in the sub-stream were intelligent and possessed more insight: the thinking minority. Now, I'm no longer convinced of this tidy conceptualisation. It's more complex than that. Not all mainstream is bad at all, while in the sub-stream, potential monsters may be lurking! As Tolstoy points out, the herd instinct is justified in accepting a 'basic way of living', particularly when a change for improvement is proposed and proves to be no improvement at all. Likewise with revolutions, where the newly installed regime becomes worse than the regime it has replaced.

As a cautious generalisation, I think it safe to say that a majority/minority division in society is an unavoidable reality. The herd instinct, for better or for worse, will see to that, for it is deceptive and volatile. Grounded in common sense, yet susceptible to every whim; imbued with communal spirit, yet blinded with personal gain; calm in the regularity of daily life, yet upset in the face of change. As of its constituent parts, the herd instinct contains both good and bad qualities in equal measure. These may, in turn, determine the direction or course the herd will take. An outcome not always easy to predict. And certainly not always towards the *future*, as the advocates of progress would have us believe… ain't necessarily so.

But whatever the direction taken, when common practice has left off to do good, or just blindly follows a trend, commitment is put to the test. Do we join in or not? The herd instinct may have no qualms and just run its course, taking casualties on board. But the outsider, what does he do? He may want to turn a blind eye, or, like the fool on the hill, stay well-clear of the 'madding crowd'. Yet, he can't help but see it all and wish to limit the collateral damage. The only difference is in the amount; will he try saving them all, or just a few? Whatever choice he makes, and his degree of self-knowledge in helping him make it, here at least, is a definite purpose: *to examine his own behaviour and that of the society he belongs to, upon the scales of justice; and, if judged necessary, to respond accordingly, thereby making use of the talents he has been given.*

There are countless examples showing this can be done. Tony and Brian are up there among them, and it is my privilege to have been closely acquainted with them both.

'But to love is the great amulet which makes the world a garden.'

R.L. Stevenson, Travels with a Donkey

Chapter Seven
The Long Way Home

Still sitting on my hill under the same foolish summer hat, I find the world has passed me by, or rather, I have moved along some six chapters. Now, the bottle of good wine needs refilling, while I inhale the scent of my sweet rose that reminds me of her loving company and our stimulating search for answers. But this romantic dreamer, with a glass too many, has forgotten his earlier, irresponsible cry, 'who cares about answers when all is good here in paradise?', and is now uncertain whether he can even read the lees at the bottom of his glass!

And if he could peer into the fated dregs, what would he see? Freud, trying to exorcise our old reptilian brain, in the firm belief that this relic is the obstacle to a more civilised state; or Marx, proclaiming the new social Gospel, in which all class struggle has been overcome; or Darwin, hanging from a tree in order to better understand the antics of his predecessors; or Nietzsche, abandoned now that God is dead, with only his tightrope acrobatics to save him; or perhaps, less ambitious, he might just see himself as he really is: a fool on the hill, with some talents and a story to tell.

A story that started as a kid, growing up in post-war England, who asked who he was and what he was doing here. A story of a youth, in search of somewhere to belong, from a home that wasn't a home at all, just a place to grow up and among people he didn't really understand. A story of a young man, thirsting for love and recognition, in a world without meaning or purpose. A story that has since become a journey, an incredible 'long and winding road'[65] with an amazing woman, the end of which… well, perhaps there is no end, at least not while I live and carry on with the search for answers.

Meeting Tony was the best thing that ever happened to me (sorry, Brian, hope you'll settle for second best!). She gave me love and recognition and showed me the way to meaning and purpose; in short, she saved an ailing plant, God bless her! But my suffering was not just *psychological*, as in a hangover from my upbringing. It was *existential* too, being related to a vague sense of 'cultural drift', or *alienation* as it is more often referred to. Tony recognised this and administered both equally; love and attention to the first, and spiritual guidance to the second. It was this dual aspect that made me realise that home is not only where the heart is but also where the *hearth* is, i.e. heart and hearth are complementary elements of the concept of belonging. One without the other will simply not do. But again, I'm getting ahead of myself.

So, the search continues. But before bringing this story to a suitable conclusion or a final 'wrapping up', the reader will allow me to indulge myself in sharing some more wisdom of others and to look a little closer at the phenomenon *Weltschmerz* and the ailing plants' dilemma.

The term *Weltschmerz* was first used by the German writer, Jean Paul Richter (1763–1825) to describe the melancholy felt in a world perceived as imperfect (the romantic view). In 1897, the French sociologist Emile Durkheim came up with a synonym,

---

65   J. Lennon/P. McCartney, *The Long and Winding Road* (1970).

'anomie' (alienation), claiming this as the chief cause of suicide within society. *Weltschmerz*, or *anomie*, is thus a symptom of the mismatch between individuals and their society, observable in the estrangement or alienation of one from the other and often marked by apathy or discontent.[66] Discontent, in itself, is not new. What is new, arguably, is the *increase* of those suffering from it. As a *cautious* generalisation, *anomie* is a by-product of the civil society that has emerged and, as such, one of the 'evils' of the modern age.

This emergent civil society is part of a larger civilisation process that began way back in the previous millennium, significant benchmarks being the Renaissance and the Industrial Revolution. According to David Riesman, these have 'in the last four hundred years, cut us off pretty decisively from the family and clan-oriented traditional ways of life in which mankind has existed throughout most of history'.[67] And, another author adds, it was the new, incumbent technologies – the heavy-wheeled plough, field rotation, watermills and windmills, print press, the compass, coal, steamships and trains – that led to 'the reorganization of space and time in the early modern era' which, he continues, 'wreaked havoc on the institutions of medieval Europe. The Church, feudal economy, and warrior kingdoms… eventually gave way to three new institutions – modern science, the market economy, and the nation-state'.[68] On the absolute monarchy, the precursor of the nation-state, Sabine and Thorson note that 'men were more prone to take pride in the national monarchies which it helped to found, than to grieve for the medieval institutions which it destroyed'.[69]

---

66 A Dutch online multimedia platform (slow television), which has broadcasted social criticism since 2014, goes by the name of *Café Weltschmerz,* thereby publicly acknowledging Weltschmerz as a *social* symptom.
67 *The Lonely Crowd*, 6.
68 Jeremy Rifkin, *The European Dream*, 94–96.
69 *A History of Political Theory*, 313.

In pursuing the civilisation process, these institutions, consciously or otherwise, 'cut off', 'wreaked havoc' and even 'destroyed' the age-old arrangements. With Tolstoy, we may grieve at this loss, or we may follow Marx, Freud, Darwin and all the adherents of evolutionary progress and praise the 'advancement' made in scientific learning, welfare and stability. But whatever our stance, we cannot ignore the *reality* of alienation. Shrugging our shoulders and passing it off as collateral damage will not make the 'uncomfortable truth' go away. So, just how successful are we in dealing with it?

In his recent book, with an evocative but highly unquotable title (call me old-fashioned!), Mark Manson gives us his own twist on the plight of the contemporary world.[70] From a background in psychology and philosophy, he has some pertinent insights to share. In fact, in the first chapter, I thought I'd already found a kindred spirit who had embarked on a similar journey. Thus, he states, in a manner reminiscent of Marx:

'An irrational sense of hopelessness is spreading across the rich, developed world. It's a paradox of progress: the better things get, the more anxious and desperate we all seem to feel'.[71]

And in the notes supporting this claim, we read that 'pessimism is widespread in the wealthy, developed world', and 'studies done in more than 132 countries show that the wealthier a country becomes, the more its population struggles with feelings of meaning and purpose'.[72]

Well, this sounds promising. He sees our ailing plants struggling with meaning or purpose and has not given up on hope, as the subtitle hints. Yet, his paradox of progress is only a paradox if we accept the definition of wealth as *material* welfare only and disregard *well-being*. Include the latter, and it's not a paradox at all, just an uncomfortable truth: 'things' may have

---

70 *Everything is F*cked: A Book About Hope.*
71 Ibid, 16.
72 Ibid, 15–16, (notes 8 and 9, page 237–238).

been getting better *materially*, but they have also been getting worse, *socially*! (This is the criticism that John Ruskin levelled at the political economists of his day, which we noted earlier). Evidently, our starting point, despite the common focus on 'meaning and purpose', is not the same at all.

At the end of part one, he states his position and intention quite clearly:

'The second half of this book is also an honest look at the modern world and everything that is fucked with it. It's an evaluation done in the hope not of fixing it, but of coming to love it. Because we must break out of our cycle of religious conflict. We must emerge from our ideological cocoons… We must stretch beyond our conception of good and evil. We must learn to love what *is*'.[73]

Well, there you have it in a nutshell. A fine example of playing to the home crowd or howling with the pack. We're done with religion, done with politics, just the individual left to accept life as it is; embrace it and love it – *amor fati* (sorry reader, you'll have to look that up). But we can't just let him flounder; no, he's thrown a lifeline in the form of *honesty*, *courage* and *humility*! Essential – can't do without those. And, almost forgot, in order to 'build and maintain hope', he needs three things: a 'sense of control', a 'belief in the value of something' and a 'community'. That last one's a bit tricky. So, we just 'restyle' it into something more neutral: 'relatedness', which means 'being part of a group that values the same things we do'! And as for values, this means finding 'something important enough to work toward'. Anything will do, and the examples the author gives are revealing: 'raising their kids well', 'saving the environment', 'making a bunch money', 'having a big-ass boat' or simply, 'improving their golf swing'; to this, he adds that writing his book is his *hope*; at least it 'gets me up in the morning'! And the language, well, the

---

73   Ibid, 129–130.

author is obviously addressing an audience used to having the 'f' word in every other sentence. This may have helped him onto the bestseller list, but how it helps improve the quality of life... hmm, not so sure.

In all fairness, Mark Manson does deliver some good Yankee punches! He exhorts us to face the 'pain of existence' with honesty and courage; to realise that much of what the market economy has to offer plays to what we want and not what we need; that 'the only logical way to improve the world is through improving ourselves – by growing up and becoming more virtuous'; in short, 'don't hope for better. Just *be* better'.

So, ailing plants, pick yourselves up and walk. You can do it, bro, just believe in yourself and take in a good breath of American faith, positive thinking, man – you're the boss! Yes, Manson says, let me put it to you again:

'There are two ways to heal yourself – that is, to replace old, faulty values, with better healthier values. The first is to re-examine the experiences of your past and rewrite the narratives around them. [...]. The other way to change your values is to begin writing the narratives of your future self, to envision what life *would* be like if you had certain values or possessed a certain identity. [...] without developing a clear vision of the future we desire... we are forever doomed to repeat the failures of our past pain'.[74]

Changing values and *rewriting narratives*, can't make it simpler than that. Maturity is just an exercise in positive psychology. This is an outcome that goes back to Freud. Not just Manson speaking here, not a rose on the dunghill or fool on the hill, but just one of the crowd of social scientists – psychologists – who believe that the individual can be 'fixed'. Just strip him of religion, politics and community, and treat him as the naked ailing plant that he is. Add a dose of breezy American optimism,

---

74 Ibid, 68–70.

and the cure is complete. Of course, the reality of 'existential pain' is not denied. Indeed, 'most people are not and probably never were equipped to live comfortably in an existential void where they must create their own values and meanings'.[75] Yet, the task at hand is to develop a mature personality, which may be 'a matter of finding something worthwhile we can do well and staking our place in the world on it'.[76]

In their enthusiasm, these positive thinkers have reduced *anomie* to a *psychological* tautology: start smiling, and the world will smile too! Social ills remedied on a personal level.

The reader will forgive this counterpunch from the Old World. I'm all for a positive attitude, to 'look on the bright side', but all this emphasis on *progress*, specifically, 'science' and the 'individual', just doesn't work for me – too easy, too mainstream. And what of *community*, that awkward issue of 'our place in the world'? Has it been brushed aside and just left to the individual to deal with? I mean, 'being part of a group that values the same things we do', how hollow is that? Social engineering par excellence!

One reason for this, according to Rifkin, who doesn't share Manson's humour or breezy optimism, is the difference between the European and American outlook on life. He notes that:

'The idea of a lone, self-reliant individual freely roaming across an endless frontier even today makes little sense to Europeans. [...] Americans covet exclusive space. Each person strives to be self-contained and autonomous. [...] Europeans seek inclusive space – being part of extended communities, including family, kin, ethnic, and class affiliation. [...] For Americans, time is future-directed and viewed as a tool to explore new opportunities. For Europeans, time is more past – and present-oriented and used to reaffirm and nurture relationships. [...] Some commentators have said that "Americans are from Mars

---

75   Peele & Brodsky, *Love and Addiction*, 142.
76   Ibid, 235.

and Europeans are from Venus" – that on a very fundamental level, we think so differently that neither can truly understand the thinking of the other'.[77]

This context allows Rifkin, when looking at discontent in society – in particular, the political unrest of the seventies and eighties – to identify 'two cross-cutting currents':

'The first, a restless yearning for some kind of higher personal calling in what was perceived to be an increasingly materialistically oriented world; the second, the need to find some sense of shared community in a society grown remote and uncaring'.[78]

In his search for a way out, he leans towards the European view, 'with its emphasis on inclusivity, diversity, quality of life, sustainability, deep play, universal human rights and the rights of nature', as being 'attractive to a generation anxious to be globally connected *and at the same time* locally embedded'.[79] [Italics added.]

This sympathetic attempt at synthesis, to bridge the cosmopolitan and parochial, aims at searing the festering wound of alienation. Yet despite its attempt to 'rescue' the individual, to bolster the ailing plant, the *causes* of discontent still remain. Thus, a guide on *how* to 'bring up children well' is still not standard issue to parents (this was Tony's major bugbear), because in our individualistic society, the nuclear family is ordained inviolate. *How* to maintain a parochial community in a global world, while discussed, is beyond our grasp, because a 'global world' is no longer large enough to entertain such communities! And *how* to find a 'healthier social life' seems more nostalgic than any actual reality, because our present life has sacrificed 'conviviality'[80] on the altar of economic progress!

---

77 *The European Dream*, 91.
78 Ibid, 2.
79 Ibid, 358.
80 Ivan Illich, *Tools for Conviviality* (New York, 1973), 12: Illich uses this term technically 'to designate a modern society of responsibly limited tools'.

Thus, while the ailing plant is immersed in his search for a more *positive* attitude, the fool on the hill shakes his head. He sees the former swallowing a medicine believing it to be beneficial. Yet, the real dilemma for the ailing plant is *which* medicine to take: that offered by the mainstream, for the mainstream or that offered by the sub-stream, for the brave-hearted!

The difficulty here is twofold. On the one hand lies the *cause* of the ailment (psychological and/or existential), and on the other, the actual *position* of the ailing plant – where does he stand? Does he lean towards mainstream and embrace progress, in which case his medicine will be the devouring of as many bestsellers as possible (!), for he has an unshakeable faith in the rational benefits of science; in the comforts afforded by the market economy; and in the 'established' order of the nation-state. A point in hand is the Covid-19 pandemic which was raging while I was writing this book. Whether from a calculated strategy or just panic football, the lockdown measures enforced by most governments were based on the assumption that this virus *must be contained*, and all further hope was set upon mass vaccination. Though the effectiveness or necessity of these measures were questioned, there was broad consensus in their acceptance. (It is ironic that the damage caused by these measures has done more to dislocate or disrupt society than the terrorist activities of the past thirty years!)

Or will he dare to listen to his conscience, question the herd instinct and refuse to live according to the opinions of others and seek a firm footing, with a little help from a friend? This is no easy choice. In fact, the choice may not be a conscious one at all, but rather an intuitive leap in the dark. Indeed, there are some who would argue that the very process of civilisation has made our intuitive faculty redundant, thus making important life choices more a leap of faith.[81]

---

81 *Civilisation and its Discontents*: Freud argued that 'hostility' towards civilisation was due to the 'sublimation of instinct', which in turn resulted in the abundance of modern-day 'neuroses'.

We recall here Tony's view on the ethical and material motivation of our actions, that 'doing the good or right thing is the chief aim in life'. For her, this was fundamental, as, I believe, it is for us all. But what is the consequence of this for the ailing plant? He is consumed with apathy and discontent, is torn between either following his own views or that of others *and* expected to choose constantly between good and evil and between higher and baser motives.

Here too, the difficulty is twofold. On the one hand, his genetic code, on the other, the social environment: *nature* versus *nurture*. There are ailing plants who, despite a deflated upbringing and depressing environment, are nevertheless able to maintain (moral) uprightness and not let the surroundings get the better of them. Nature has apparently equipped them with a survival kit. Others are less fortunate. They are tossed into the world and struggle to stay afloat. Where do they set course if they have neither heart nor hearth to guide them?

They may cast their eyes about them and consider the options. As adolescents, says Margaret Mead, 'our children grow up to find a world of choices dazzling their unaccustomed eyes. In religion they may be Catholics, Protestants, Christian Scientists, Spiritualists, Agnostics, Atheists, or even pay no attention at all to religion'.[82] Thus, she continues, in a passage worth quoting in full:

'Our young people are faced by a series of different groups which believe different things and advocate different practices, and to each of which some trusted friend or relative may belong. So a girl's father may be a Presbyterian, an imperialist, a vegetarian, a teetotaller, with a strong literary preference for Edmund Burke, a believer in the open shop and a high tariff, who believes that women's place is in the home, that young girls should wear corsets, not roll their stockings, not smoke, nor go riding with young men in the evening. But her mother's father may be a Low

---

82   *Coming of Age in Samoa*, 161.

Episcopalian, a believer in high living, a strong advocate of States' Rights and the Monroe Doctrine, who reads Rabelais, likes to go to musical shows and horse races. Her aunt is an agnostic, an ardent advocate of women's rights, an internationalist who rests all her hopes on Esperanto, is devoted to Bernard Shaw, and spends her spare time in campaigns of anti-vivisection. Her elder brother, whom she admires exceedingly, has just spent two years at Oxford. He is an Anglo-Catholic, an enthusiast concerning all things medieval, writes mystical poetry, reads Chesterton, and means to devote his life to seeking for the lost secret of medieval stained glass. Her mother's younger brother is an engineer, a strict materialist, who never recovered from reading Haeckel in his youth; he scorns art, believes that science will save the world, scoffs at everything that was said and thought before the nineteenth century, and ruins his health by experiments in the scientific elimination of sleep. Her mother is of a quietist frame of mind, very much interested in Indian philosophy, a pacifist, a strict non-participator in life, who in spite of her daughter's devotion to her will not make any move to enlist her enthusiasms. And this may be within the girls own household. Add to it the groups represented, defended, advocated by her friends, her teachers, and the books which she reads by accident, and the list of possible enthusiasms, of suggested allegiances, incompatible with one another, becomes appalling'.[83]

Confronted with this 'dazzling' array, the alienated plant has only his idling *intuition* to help him. His personality must find somewhere to grow and to flower, and this must be managed somehow. The first task is to find out *who* he really is. This may sound ridiculous, but in modern, urban society, it is not. In his novel, *The Europeans*, Henry James aptly presents this question of identity in an engaging conversation between the American and European cousins, Gertrude and Felix:

---

83 Ibid, 162–163.

"'I don't believe you know my name,' he said. 'I am called Felix Young. Your father is my uncle. My mother was his half-sister, and older than he.'

'Yes,' said Gertrude, 'and she turned Roman Catholic and married in Europe.'

'I see you know,' said the young man. 'She married, and she died. Your father's family didn't like her husband. They called him a foreigner; but he was not. My poor father was born in Sicily, but his parents were American.'

'In Sicily?' Gertrude murmured.

'It is true,' said Felix Young, 'that they had spent their lives in Europe. But they were very patriotic. And so are we.'

'And you are Sicilian,' said Gertrude.

'Sicilian, no! Let's see. I was born at a little place – a dear little place – in France. My sister was born at Vienna.'

'So you are French,' said Gertrude.

'Heaven forbid!' cried the young man. Gertrude's eyes were fixed upon him almost instantly. He began to laugh again. 'I can easily be French, if that will please you.'

'You are a foreigner of some sort,' said Gertrude.

'Of some sort – yes; I suppose so. But who can say of what sort? I don't think we have ever had occasion to settle the question. You know there are people like that. About their country, their religion, their profession, they can't tell.'

Gertrude stood there gazing; she had not asked him to sit down. She had never heard of people like that; she wanted to hear. 'Where do you live?' she asked.

'They can't tell that either!' said Felix. 'I'm afraid you will think we are little better than vagabonds. I have lived anywhere – everywhere. I really think I have lived in every city in Europe.'"[84]

Despite the humour, James's observation on identity cuts as deep as any scientific analysis. For one species of alienated plants

---

84   *The Europeans*, 27–28.

– (im)migrants – the whole question is particularly harrowing. In a novel considered controversial, Salmon Rushdie describes their plight thus:

'... mingling with the remnants of the plane, equally fragmented, equally absurd, there floated the debris of the soul, broken memories, sloughed-off selves, severed mother tongues, violated privacies, untranslatable jokes, extinguished futures, lost loves, the forgotten meaning of hollow, booming words, land, belonging, home'.[85]

The alienated person may eventually discover *who* he is, yet still must reconcile this with *where* to belong. He picks up another book, this time on sociology. Among its contributors, he finds Ferdinand Tönnies (1855–1936), a contemporary of Durkheim who has gone to some length in distinguishing between *community* (*Gemeinschaft*) and *society* (*Gesellschaft*) and their characteristics. He reads:

'In the city as well as in the capitol, and especially in the metropolis, family life is decaying. The more and longer their influence prevails, the more the residuals of family life acquire a purely accidental character. For there are only few who will confine their energies within such a narrow circle; all are attracted outside by business, interests, and pleasures, and thus separated from one another'.[86]

He sighs and recalls Marcel Proust's remark that 'what brings men together is not a community of views but a consanguinity of minds'.[87] How different from Manson's neutral definition of 'being part of a group that values the same things we do'! But where are we going with this? Where then, does the ailing plant turn to for support? Ah, of course, Margaret Mead, who has said so much about growing up, surely she can help? Yes, here it is:

'We may realize that it is not civilization, in the sense of

---

85 *The Satanic Verses*, 4.
86 Marcello Truzzi, *Sociology: The Classic Statements*, 152.
87 *Remembrance of Things Past: 1*, 470.

modern urbanisation, alone that has alienated human beings from the rhythm of their own bodies. Between the period when our foraging ancestors could be trusted to spit out at once an evil-tasting berry… and today… human beings have fumbled, eagerly, imaginatively, clumsily, at the problem of fitting a man-made way of life upon an organism that has the skill to design such ways of life but no automatic capacity to fit them on. [...] Men have travelled the same road; and none of it has been natural. [...] Our problem is not to be natural, which would mean in effect to strip off every vestige of civilization, abandon speech, and return to an animal life; [...] Our problem is to develop and elaborate this new method of evolution…'[88]

But, oh dear, what's this she's saying? That our alienation is not *only* due to modern civilisation, which is undeniable, but that we have, in fact, from the very beginning, been 'fumbling' along in our attempt to create an *un*natural, or 'man-made way of life'. Well, let's take a breath here! She clearly believes in evolution, though it is not of the usual linear variety, as in progressing from a natural state to a civilised one. All ideas of returning to a 'natural' state, she qualifies as 'sentimental nonsense', for this state has never existed! She seems to be arguing that, because our human nature is unclear – somewhere between the beasts and angels – all we can do is 'fumble' along and try to 'develop and elaborate this new method of evolution'. In fact, without a guidebook or compass, we have hardly progressed at all. Now, there's a comforting thought. This is the sort of evolution I prefer!

It reminds me of Proust's earlier remark that we are born into the world without any knowledge of the moral precepts placed in our hearts. That an unseen 'moving finger' shapes our destiny, that 'even in the most insignificant details of our daily life, none of us can be said to constitute a material whole [...] our social

---

88 *Male and Female*, 223–224.

personality is a creation of the thoughts of other people'.[89] How far removed is this imaginative surrealism from the hard realism of science?

A step further, and we enter the realm of mysticism. Close your eyes, and consider these mystic words from the poem, *Lines Composed a Few Miles above Tintern Abbey,* by William Wordsworth:

> *'That blessed mood*
> *In which the burthen of the mystery,*
> *In which the heavy and weary weight*
> *Of all this unintelligible world,*
> *Is lightened, that serene and blessed mood*
> *In which the affections gently lead us on,*
> *Until, the breath of this corporeal frame*
> *And even the motion of our human blood*
> *Almost suspended, we are laid asleep*
> *In body, and become a living soul:*
> *While, with an eye made quiet by the power*
> *Of harmony, and the deep power of joy,*
> *We see into the life of things'.*

Now, this certainly is a possible alternative. However, according to Karen Armstrong, mysticism has been 'regarded with some suspicion by many Jews and Muslims' while:

'In the West, mysticism has never been a mainstream religious enthusiasm. The Protestant and Catholic Reformers either outlawed or marginalised it and the scientific Age of Reason did not encourage this mode of perception'.

Nevertheless, she explains:

'Mystics often insist that human beings must deliberately create this sense of God for themselves, with the same degree

---

89   *Remembrance of Things Past: 1*, 20.

of care and attention that others devote to artistic creation, [to] cultivate their sense of the wonder and ineffable significance of life'.[90]

The writer, Romain Rolland, described this 'sense of wonder', in a letter to Freud, as 'oceanic' – a feeling of an indissoluble bond, of being one with the external world as a whole. This was his response to Freud, who had sent him a small book that treated religion as an illusion. He said that he was 'sorry that I [Freud] had not properly appreciated the true source of religious sentiments' and that this 'peculiar feeling, which he himself is never without... he would like to call a sensation of eternity', which, he adds, 'is a purely subjective fact, not an article of faith.' To this, Freud admits, 'I cannot discover this "oceanic" feeling in myself. It is not easy to deal scientifically with feelings. [...] I could not convince myself of the primary nature of such a feeling. But this gives me no right to deny that it does in fact occur in other people'.[91]

Freud, hard-headed scientist as he is, clearly doesn't *buy into* this 'mode of perception'. And he is not alone. In a world no longer dominated by religion, but by science, 'many people today', says Armstrong, 'seem to have lost the will to make this imaginative effort'. She painfully concludes:

'The aimlessness, alienation, *anomie* and violence that characterises so much of modern life seems to indicate that now that they are not deliberately creating a faith in 'God' or anything else – it matters little what – many people are falling into despair'.[92]

And our ailing plant too, is still despairing. For what, finally, can we offer him? Will mysticism tempt him, in the knowledge that this is neither for the multitude nor for the faint-hearted?

---

90 *A History of God*, 454–456 (the arguments on these pages I have paraphrased).
91 *Civilisation and its Discontents*, 1–2.
92 *A History of God*, 456.

Tony had a soft spot for the mystics, especially the bible prophets, but, aware of mainstream sentiment, she publicly promoted 'upbringing' as the safer choice and gave it her best shot!

If mysticism proves too demanding or obscure, there is always the trendy and less-demanding alternative: biological evolution. That bugging question, 'what on earth am I going to do?' now becomes, 'what am I doing on earth?' There, it now seems, he will learn that man is 'on the point of developing into that animal species' that 'would appear like a process of biological mutation in which human bodies gradually begin to be covered by shells of steel'.[93]

If this sounds like science-fiction, Mark Manson's telescopic vision is even more promising:

'AI [artificial intelligence] is coming [...] AI will reach a point where its intelligence outstrips ours by so much that we will no longer comprehend what it's doing [...] We are a self-hating, self-destructing species. That is not a moral statement; it's simply a fact. This internal tension we all feel, all the time? That's what got us here. It's what got us to this point. It's our arms race. And we're about to hand over the evolutionary baton to the defining information processors of the next epoch: the machines [...] So, allow me to say that I, for one, welcome our AI overlords [...] These algorithms make our lives better. They make our lives more efficient. They make *us* more efficient. That's why, as soon as we cross over, there's no going back [...] I believe artificial intelligence is Nietzsche's "something greater"'[94]

Well, if Nietzsche were to read this, I'm sure he would lose his balance, fall from his tightrope and now be lying prostrate on the floor of the abyss. Stone dead but with a wry grin on his face!

But still the ailing plant is not convinced. Surely, there must be some firmer ground to pitch camp on? The conundrum is that

---

93   Hannah Arendt, *The Human Condition*, 322–323.
94   *Everything is F*cked*, 218–227 (I have paraphrased his presentation of these ideas).

he knows *what* he yearns for, but at best can only resolve it on a personal level. Because he knows that *part* of the malady is his inability to affirm life, to say yea, in spite of all feelings and signs to the contrary. That it all boils down to an 'appetite for fruitful activity and a high quality of life'.[95]

And his instinct tells him, or rather vaguely prompts him, he also needs a *community*, but he is unable to find it. What he sees around him are substitutes – modern science, the market economy and the nation-state – not the real thing. How he would love to change the world! He could find a fellow reformer, John Ruskin perhaps, who spent his whole life 'persuading the middle classes to abandon the economics and social morality of the market'. And not succumb, as Ruskin finally did, 'to feel the immensity of the task and to see the evils of the modern age as irreversible'.[96]

Or if not a community, then perhaps, by default, there is still a 'tradition' to be salvaged. By this, says Jaroslav Pelikan, we mean 'the living faith of the dead', as opposed to 'the dead faith of the living'. 'When we learn to interact with the "tradition", [...] we do acquire the "insight"' necessary to keep the tradition alive. To make his point, Pelikan concludes with his own translation of a quote from Goethe's *Faust*:

'What you have as heritage,
Take now as task;
For thus you will make it your own!'[97]

Community, tradition, heritage – the ailing plant is now gasping for breath. Yet, somehow, also breathing more freely.

---

95 G.B. Shaw, *Prefaces* (cited in C. Wilson, *Religion and the Rebel*, (Bath, 1984) 254).
96 *Unto This Last and Other Writings*, 31 (quoted from the introduction by Clive Wilmer).
97 *The Vindication of Tradition* (New Haven, 1984), 81–82.

He understands that without pedigree, he is but debris drifting through the universe – free yes, but lost and longing for somewhere, or someone, to latch on to, a place to call home. We hear his lament, oh, please, 'take me home, country roads'![98] If only we could give him a one-way ticket to paradise. But perhaps he may get lucky and find his own 'rose on a dunghill'. Or at second best, he'll meet another plant and one less ailing than he. Together, they will cope with life while struggling with the meaning of it.

Whatever choice he makes, he knows he must trust his instinct and his conscience to help him make the right one. At least he now knows his purpose: *to examine his own behaviour and that of the 'society' he belongs to, upon the scales of justice; and, if judged necessary, to respond accordingly, thereby making use of the talents he has been given.*

---

[98] John Denver, 'Take Me Home, Country Roads' (1971).

'Wisdom found no place where she might dwell.'

The Book of Enoch

Chapter Eight

Amor Fati

From the vantage point of my hill, I now finally reflect on how this enterprise has worked out. The primary purpose of this book was to pay tribute to my dearest Tony *and* to share our reflections, both hers and mine, on the meaning of life. I have endeavoured to show her love and wisdom and portrayed her as a 'healthy plant' who, unconditionally, helped save an ailing one. If I am now able to cope with life, it is chiefly due to her love and inspiration. Though I still enjoy a bottle of good wine, it is no longer a prerequisite to remind me of her loving company and our enduring search for answers. I am drunken with her sweet scent and have imbibed her spirit to the full. She, as the song goes, was a lady,[99] and I but a fool. And, romantic dreamer that I am, I now cry out, amidst a flood of tears, that all is good here in paradise!

And, wallowing in paradise, I have reflected on the wisdom of others and come to realise that the puzzle still remains: our origin is debatable, our nature unclear and our purpose still

---

99 Peter Skellern, 'You're a Lady' (1973).

under review. On our journey towards this realisation, we have discovered some truths, both remarkable and fascinating, but do they provide answers? No. At best, they bear witness to the mystery of life and reaffirm the continual search for meaning. That quest remains an open book, to which Tony and I have contributed.

And now, this fool on the hill has to somehow close the story. I have portrayed Tony as open and spontaneous and highlighted her observant and serene character. We have witnessed her love of children and the importance she attached to their upbringing; this, she believed, was fundamental in establishing a 'firm footing' in order better to cope with life. And lastly, but most importantly, we noted her insistence on making the most of one's talents and applying these to doing the 'good or right thing' in life. Doing what is 'good', with its ethical implications, was her moral compass.

These, I believe, are the principal aspects of her personality and wisdom that define her stance in life, both as an outsider and seeker of the truth. But if we are to fully understand her, we must not neglect the *Christian* factor. Indeed, this tribute would not be complete without further reference to Tony's religious views and the central place the *Bible* and its wisdom occupied in her life.

Though she read widely and loved learning, it was always the *Bible* that she turned to for answers and consolation. For her, the *Bible* was the ultimate test, the touchstone and companion of all her soul-searching. She studied its contents and many commentaries related to it, from the canonical Scriptures to Apocalyptic Literature, such as the *Book of Enoch*. This book was a favourite source, and the sentence quoted at the top of this page must have struck a chord, as she copied it onto the front page of her edition! The appeal of this work clearly suggests that she too, shared the Christian view that life on earth is nothing but *misère*, that 'for such a world there was no remedy, only destruction; if the good were ever to triumph it must be in a new world'.[100] Thus, the *Book of Enoch* begins:

'The words of the blessing of Enoch, wherewith he blessed the elect and righteous, who will be living in the day of tribulation, when all the wicked and godless are to be removed'.[101]

And the 'wicked and godless', who stupidly follow their own selfish needs, whether alone or collectively, can only expect to incur the wrath of God:

'The fool hath said in his heart, *there is* no God. They are corrupt, they have done abominable works, *there is* none that doeth good. The Lord looked down from heaven upon the children of men, to see if there were any that did understand, *and* seek God. They are *all* gone aside, they are altogether become filthy: *there is* none that doeth good, no, not one'.[102]

The idea of heaven – a place reserved for the blessed (elect and righteous) after life, *on condition* of their having done *good* while on earth and of following God's commandments – is a fundamental element of Christian doctrine. Tony rejected this, or rather, she contented herself to do good in this life *regardless* of whether she would or would not be admitted to heaven. She *may* have privately wished it, and even considered it a pleasant prospect, but, to my knowledge, it was never a conscious driving motive and certainly not foremost in her prayers. What mattered for her was doing good, *here and now*. This is an important distinction in appreciating her religious attitude. She could speculate on life hereafter, yet her heart reached out to the present. It was not the promise of an 'everlasting life' that motivated her, but rather to live out her promise to do good in *this* life. She believed in the *living* Christian ethic, over and above pure doctrine.

To show charity and to love one's neighbour was, for her, the true path in life. But this requires self-sacrifice and wisdom.

---

100   *The Book of Enoch*, viii (introduction).
101   *Idem*, 31.
102   *Psalm XIV*, 1–3.

The former, Tony had in abundance, the latter, she found in the *Bible*. Not so much as disseminated by the Catholic Church, but through the *prophets*. These, as we noted earlier, were her heroes. She found solace and inspiration in their transcendental views on God and a just society. The books of *Daniel*, *Isaiah*, *Ezekiel* and *Jeremiah* and the *Book of Psalms* were her staple diet, which she consumed and sublimated.

While many in atheistic Western European culture move progressively away from God and religion, Tony chose to hold on to her faith. Yes, she too had her doubts, particularly on the lack of 'divine intervention' in the face of the genocide of the Jews and the role of the Catholic Church during World War II, but her overriding belief in the Christian ethic remained intact. Indeed, she unfailingly put its principles and wisdom into practice, as I now briefly hope to show.

If, as lamented above, wisdom can find no 'dwelling place' among men then, Tony would argue, we must prove the contrary and try our best to accommodate it:

'For all our days are passed away in thy wrath: we spend our years as a tale that is told [...] so teach us to number our days, that we may apply our hearts unto wisdom'.[103]

This exhortation – to apply our hearts unto wisdom – was one of Tony's favourites and lies at the core of her philosophy. If we fail to incorporate this into our lives, we miss the opportunity of greater fulfilment and 'fruitful activity' and are left to reflect upon whatever fate may record:

'The Moving Finger writes;
And having writ,
Moves on: nor all thy Piety nor
Wit
Shall lure it back to cancel half

---

[103] *Psalm XC*, 9–12.

A Line,
Nor all thy Tears wash out a word
of it'.[104]

Thus, although he is a hard taskmaster, we must realise that:

'The fear of the Lord is the beginning of wisdom: a good understanding have all they that do his commandments: his praise endureth forever'.[105]

And his commandments are pure, simple and unambiguous:

'What man *is he that* desireth life, *and* loveth *many* days, that he may see good? Keep thy tongue from evil, and thy lips from speaking guile. Depart from evil, and do good; seek peace, and pursue it'.[106]

We are also reminded that:

'The face of the Lord *is* against them that do evil, to cut off the remembrance of them from the earth. *The righteous* cry, and the Lord heareth, and delivereth them out of all their troubles. The Lord *is* nigh unto them that are of a broken heart; and saveth such as be of a contrite spirit'.[107]

Only with a contrite spirit and in following the commandments, can a righteous man say:

'I have not sat with vain persons, neither will I go in with dissemblers. I have hated the congregation of evil doers: and will not sit with the wicked. I will wash my hands in innocency'.[108]

And we all know how difficult this is, '*he who hath no sin, let him cast the first stone*'.[109] Yet, Tony did somehow retain a childlike innocence. She believed in prayer and the mercy of God:

'For his anger *endureth but* a moment; in his favour *is* life: weeping may endure for a night, but joy *cometh* in the morning'.[110]

---

104 *The Rubáiyát*, Stanza LI.
105 *Psalm CXI*, 10.
106 *Psalm XXXIV*, 12–14.
107 *Idem*, 16–18.
108 *Psalm XXVI*, 4–6.
109 *John*, 8:7.
110 *Psalm XXX*, 5.

So, in a state of blessed affirmation, we should praise the Lord:

'For with thee is the fountain of life: in thy light shall we see light'.[111]

Whenever Tony was confronted with the complaining or stupidity of others, she would invariably respond with the direct remarks, "You don't pray enough," and "Count your blessings." And she always prayed daily for herself but especially for others. She said unbelievers are not aware of the power of prayer and seem unable to make the effort, and therefore she felt compelled to do it for them! This, on her part, was an unselfish act and many, on realising this, were humbled.

Here, she followed God's example:

'Who humbled himself to behold the things that are in heaven, and in the earth! He raiseth up the poor out of the dust, and lifteth the needy out of the dunghill'.[112]

The observant reader will note here the clue to part of the title of this book, and, I would add, her *raison d'être*. For, as I have witnessed her doing many times:

'A good man sheweth favour, and lendeth: He hath dispersed, he hath given to the poor'.[113]

Both at home and on holiday, Tony gave freely to the poor and needy. Not only to those begging or requesting alms but also to whoever she felt the urge to help. And not just loose change, as is the way of many, but invariably more substantial amounts, notes included.

I remember one young woman, an immigrant to the Netherlands, who worked at a local store but really hoped to start up a child day-care school. Tony befriended her and took her 'under her wing'. She gave her advice and offered to help her get started. It turned out that she had a *fiancé* who had found

---

111 *Psalm* XXXVI, 9.
112 *Psalm* CXIII, 6–7.
113 *Psalm* CXII, 5, 9.

work in France (Alsace) and he wanted her to join him. Tony said that, if she loved him, this was an excellent opportunity and encouraged her to take the plunge. She also gave her money to cover the travel expenses. She took Tony's advice, and money, and started out on her new adventure. Later, she wrote that she was happily married and expecting their first baby. Letters continued, and we received an invitation to visit them. This we did *en route* to a holiday in France and found her well and profusely thankful to Tony for all her generosity and support. Happy ending!

Speaking of holidays in France, the further south one travels, the greater the number of needy, male and female, who beg for alms. You will find them on the streets, at subways, in parks and at churches when mass begins. They place a dish or cardboard box in front of them, or just hold out their hand as you pass by. Tony always gave them money, usually full amounts (coins or notes, whatever was at hand).

"Small change," she said, "is offensive and miserly. If you wish to give alms, then your intention must be genuine and given with a warm heart."

Those receiving, recognise this. Countless times, I have witnessed their grateful responses whenever Tony stopped before them, from a vigorous nodding of the head or happy smile, to the exclamation, "God bless you." One woman, who always sat at one end of a particular subway, smiled and withdrew her hand when we passed by again, as if to say, "Thank you, you've given me enough already!"

To my chagrin, I once said to Tony that the same woman was wearing a watch, concluding that she probably wasn't as poor as she made out.

"That's beside the point," Tony reprimanded me. "If you knew she were rich but was begging nevertheless, would you not give?"

An act of charity is done in good faith, not as a judgement. It's the story of the good Samaritan – *Bible* wisdom.

A similar thing occurred many years earlier during a holiday in Portugal. Tony had given alms to an old woman who was begging outside a church. The next day, we visited Silves, a famous market town, and, to our surprise, we saw the same old woman again.

"Aha," I exclaimed. "Now we know what she used the money for!"

"Well, good on her," Tony replied and went and greeted the lady very warmly. Touched by her friendliness, the old woman gave Tony two apples and offered to show us around the market – point taken, and how lovely is that!

Tony argued that, as parents struggle with getting the right balance in the upbringing, so do adults struggle to grasp what is important in life. Many take *money* as the only measurement of value and are subsequently blinded by it.

"See for yourself," she said. "The next time you have a chat with friends or family, just put some money down on the table, even a small amount, and observe their increasing distraction and uneasiness."

I did, and she was right! To make a true valuation of what is worth in life, we must first free ourselves from the lure of greed. Money is the carrot dangling in front of our eyes. It should be used to do good not for gain. It is the story of selling out to the devil and losing one's soul – *Bible* wisdom again! I realised that Tony had freed herself from this pitfall.

Aware of the attraction money held for many, and the power of kind words, Tony often put this to good effect in hotels and restaurants. On the first day of our arrival in a hotel, she would immediately look up the head waiter or porter and, having found him, say a few words and *knowingly* shake his hand. This 'transaction' always produced the required effect, i.e. impeccable service, as if we were VIPs: a choice of table, clean and tidy room and most attentive staff.

"Never tip at the end of your stay but at the beginning,"

she said. "*And* pay compliments – that always guarantees good service!"

The most enjoyable part was again, the reaction of other guests. From incomprehension and disbelief, to envious hostility – why do they always get the best table and are pampered so? You could read their thoughts on their faces; it was fascinating to watch! What you give is what you get.

When Tony was eighty-four years old, we made a trip to Egypt. Something she had always dreamt of. It was an all-in tour, including guided excursions in Cairo, a night train to Aswan, a Nile boat to Luxor with more guided excursions and finally, back to Cairo. I mention this trip not only because it was so memorable – seeing Tony at her age on a camel and the guy helping her up keeping his hand on her leg for much longer than was necessary (OK, I was jealous, but she was still good-looking!) – but also because it affords some more illustrations of her character *and* my following her example.

At Cairo, we were picked up by the tour operator and taken to our hotel. We were the fourth couple from the Netherlands; the other three were friends and had planned this trip together. The organisers had made dining arrangements so that people from the same countries were seated together. We were thus shown to a table with the three couples we didn't know. I decided to put Tony's tactics into practice and, without telling her my plan, offered to pay the first round of drinks! This had the desired effect of breaking the ice and getting us accepted into their little group.

"Well done," Tony said later. "You're learning!"

As it turned out, they were nice people with a good sense of humour, and we all had a great time in Egypt together.

As the days passed and we got to know each other better, I was curious to see what effect Tony would have on their behaviour and also how she would handle the guides (she sometimes knew more than they did!) *and* the hordes of children who, like flies to honey, constantly badger tourists for money. She admitted to me that the latter were very annoying. It was impossible to go anywhere without being swamped by a plague of kids. And if you did give them something, they became even more insistent. Most tourists try to ignore them or brush them off, but that wasn't her style. So, one day, she beckoned them to come, crouched down to their level, took their hands and looked them in the eye. They looked back at her in anticipation, uncertain what was happening. Then, she gave the same amount of money to each one, telling them to use it wisely and go to school, instead of pestering the tourists! Later that day, we recognised some of them again, but instead of rushing up to us, they kept their distance – remarkable! Upbringing really was her thing.

At Aswan, amidst all the historic sites, lies the Old Cataract Hotel. This iconic, British colonial grand hotel was built to house European travellers, whose famous names include Winston Churchill and Princess Diana. Situated on the banks of the Nile, this idyllic resort offers luxury and the sumptuous taste of decadence of a bygone era. Of course, we couldn't leave Aswan without a glimpse of its splendour.

So, one evening after dinner, we all decided to visit the place and soak in the atmosphere, relax in the bar with an after-dinner coffee or cognac, which was probably as far as our purses would stretch! This gave me the idea of putting Tony's views on money and value to the test. While everyone sauntered through the huge lobby and found their way to the bar – which, by the way, overlooks the Nile and is by far the grandest room to relax in I've ever entered – I held back and quietly approached the reception desk to ask for some information about the hotel and even the price of the cheapest room! Armed with this information, I joined the others in the bar, ordered a cognac – which was served on a silver platter by a deferential waiter in white gloves – and prepared myself for some educational fun. Once we were settled and feeling comfortable, I asked the group to guess how much they thought the cheapest room in this hotel would cost them. Well, that put the cat among the pigeons, for they all flew off at the most exorbitant rates imaginable. Their estimates were all sky-high! With no one *under* a thousand euros per night, except one – yes, you guessed right, Tony. At five hundred euros, she was by far the nearest to the actual cost of two hundred and fifty per night! Granted, it was a back room with no view of the Nile, but had they thought of that? Were they not rather 'blinded' by the glamour of the place and their own desire of occupying a 'Churchill suite'? Money is the carrot dancing before our eyes, no matter where we are!

As the days progressed, the members of our group began to realise that Tony was a force to be reckoned with. Her knowledge of Egyptian history and art, and her kindness and generosity, began to have their effect. They started to confide in her and ask her advice on family matters, especially the women. Tony also took to wearing ancient Egyptian clothing and ornaments, which was soon emulated by the others. In the Valley of the Kings, where many tombs of the pharaohs are found, one can visit a tomb with a guide on condition of not suffering from claustrophobia! Tony had so looked forward to this, but on seeing the narrow and deep descent, her nerve failed her, and she decided to stay above ground. I was really very sorry for her, for I knew how much this meant to her.

"How wise you are, Tony," the other two women cried. "We'll stay up here with you. We didn't fancy it either but didn't dare say it until you did!"

No matter how much you desire a thing, it is sometimes more prudent to let it pass. Wisdom reveals itself not just in words but also in deeds.

At the end of our trip, we discussed the highlights and reflected on what we had enjoyed most. Tony and I thanked them for allowing us to join their group, knowing how difficult it is letting outsiders share your intimacy.

They in turn said they had enjoyed our stimulating company, and one of the women said to Tony, "You are so sweet, the classic *kind old lady* type."

It was meant as a compliment, and Tony took it full on the chin, with her characteristic, "Goh!"

I can think of no better way to end this tribute than with that exclamation. For me, that one, single word sums up all that I love in her. A sense of wonder, joy and affirmation. The innocence of a child and the wisdom of a woman, all in one. Her wisdom reverberates in my soul, to lead and guide me forever. She was my rose on a dunghill, a woman that did make a difference, to me and to all who met her.

Thus, with Tony in my heart and in honour of her memory, I end this tribute to her and to her wisdom – follow the truth, be true to yourself and put your talents to good use. This is not a burden but a reminder for one less strong than she.

I promised the reader at the beginning a good read, if nothing else. If the reader has been disappointed, then the blame is all mine. All I can humbly say is that to the mystery of life, I have added but a few silly footnotes to the writings of others more worthy of the undertaking than I.

And if, as George Bernard Shaw said, it all boils down to an 'appetite for fruitful activity and a high quality of life', then it was also he, to wrap up on a lighter note, who said that 'nothing divides people more than religion, politics and sex... so, if you want to have a congenial dinner party, then avoid these subjects'!

But if you're searching for the meaning of life, how can you?

Bibliography

Arendt, Hannah, *The Human Condition* (Chicago, 1958)
Armstrong, Karen, *A History of God* (London, 1995)
Aurelius, Marcus, *Meditations* (Harmondsworth, 1977)
Boethius, *The Consolation of Philosophy* (Harmondsworth, 1978)
Boorstin, Daniel J, *The Seekers* (New York, 1998)
Charles, R.H. (transl.), *The Book of Enoch* (1st publ. 1917, London, 1977)
Erikson, Erik, *Childhood and Society* (Granada, 1981)
Eyre, G & Spottiswoode, W, *The Holy Bible* (London, 1863)
Freud, Sigmund, *Civilization and its Discontents* (1st publ. 1930, London, 1975)
Gurdjieff, G.I. *Meetings with Remarkable Men* (1st publ. 1963, London, 1978)
Harari, Yuval Noah, *Sapiens: A Brief History of Humankind* (London, 2011)
Horney, Karen, *New Ways in Psychoanalysis* (1st publ. 1939, New York, 1966)
Horney, Karen, *Our Inner Conflicts* (1st publ. 1946, London, 1957)
James, Henry, *The Europeans* (1st publ. 1878, Harmondsworth, 1979)
James, William, *The Varieties of Religious Experience* (1st publ. 1902, New York, 1961)
Jones, Ted, *The French Riviera* (London, 2007)
Kempis, Thomas À, *The Imitation of Christ* (Harmondsworth, 1977)
Khayyám, Omar, *Rubáiyát of /* transl. Edward Fitzgerald (1st publ. 1909, London, 1973)
Lawrence, D.H. *Women in Love* (1st publ. 1921, Harmondsworth, 1977)
Manson, Mark, *Everything is F*cked: A Book About Hope* (New York, 2019)
Mead, Margaret, *Coming of Age in Samoa* (1st publ. 1928, Harmondsworth, 1981)
Mead, Margaret, *Male and Female* (1st publ. 1949,

Harmondsworth,1981)
Nietzsche, Friedrich, *Thus Spoke Zarathustra* (1st publ. 1885, Harmondsworth, 1975)
Nisbet, Robert, *The Social Philosophers* (St Albans, 1976)
Pascal, Blaise, *Pensées* (1st publ. 1662, Harmondsworth, 1977)
Peele, Stanton & Brodsky, Archie, *Love and Addiction* (London, 1977)
Proust, Marcel, *Remembrance of Things Past,* Vols 1-3 (1st publ. 1927, Harmondsworth, 1989)
Riesman, David, *The Lonely Crowd* (New Haven, 1961)
Rifkin, Jeremy, *The European Dream* (New York, 2005)
Ruskin, John, *Unto This Last and Other Writings* (1st publ. 1862, London, 1997)
Sabine, George & Thorson, Thomas, *A History of Political Theory* (Hinsdale, 1973, 4th ed)
Thoreau, Henry David, *Walden* (1849) and *Civil Disobedience* (1854), (London, 2017)
Tolstoy, Leo, *Resurrection* (1st publ. 1899, Harmondsworth, 1973)
Truzzi, Marcello (ed), *Sociology: The Classic Statements* (New York, 1971)
Wilson, Colin, *The Outsider* (1st publ. 1956, London, 1978)
Wilson, Colin, *The New Existentialism* (1st publ. 1966, London, 1980)

Acknowledgements

First and foremost, a huge and inexpressible thanks to my lifelong friend, Brian. For his unerring love and support during this difficult period. For his wise comments and tireless proofreading – page for page, chapter for chapter – which helped both me and the book stay on track! If I ever had any doubts, he never did. His continued belief in my ability to pull this off and do Tony proud ('this is what she would have wanted') gave me the strength to make the full journey. God bless you, Brian!

And also, my gratitude to Mary, Tony's favourite cousin. During the several conversations and email messages we held following Tony's death, it was the chance remark of hers – 'you have a lovely writing style, have you ever considered becoming a writer?' – that somehow confirmed my intention of writing this book. Mary did not know at the time that I was already toying with the idea of writing a tribute to Tony. Her suggestion prompted me into the realisation: 'yes, why not, I can do this'. Help can sometimes appear quite unexpectedly. So, thanks Mary; without your indirect encouragement, who knows, perhaps this book may never have materialised!

To all four of Tony's children, I am much indebted to their generosity of spirit. If they did hold any misgivings or reserves about the whole prospect of a book being written about the private life of their mother, they soon came round to sharing my enthusiasm and gave me full support. It was their express wish that I give each of them a fictitious name. Thanks guys, for your trust in this enterprise.

I also offer my thanks to all other friends and family who,

directly or indirectly, have given advice or shown support along the way. Thank you all.

Specifically, I would like to thank the whole publishing team for their professional guidance and support. With you guys on board, we have transformed a dream into a book!

Finally, last but not least, I wish to thank you, the reader, for having the courage to invest in a new story, by a new author. I hope your investment has given satisfaction, which is all I can ask for.

About the Author

John Ayress (1956) was born in Clacton, England, into a musical family, the eldest son of a classical pianist and mother a local choir singer. He spent his childhood in Bristol and later in Ware, Hertfordshire, and received a secondary, comprehensive education. A confessed autodidact with a love for history and philosophy, he also claims a modest talent for poetry, prose, drawing and musical composition. The latter he 'discovered' later on in life, and it became his overriding passion. In 2000, he recorded sixteen of his romantic piano pieces on CD, entitled 'Suite Nostalgia', in collaboration with Nobuko Takahashi, an established concert pianist.

After meeting Tony, John, then an assistant golf professional, relocated to the Netherlands and took a degree in Dutch law, followed by a basic training in mediation. During this period, John's writing abilities resurfaced to produce some unpublished work, that includes poetry and prose, and two academic articles. This book, his debut, is an engaging mix of the biographical and autobiographical, woven around the theme of the meaning of life.

John currently lives and works in the Netherlands. Contact him at: johnayress@tele2.nl

About Tony

The 'rose' of this story is Antonia. A middle-aged, attractive and intelligent Dutch woman at a crossroad in her life. During the long, hot summer of 1976, she meets, by chance or fate, the author, then a young man of twenty. He describes this encounter as 'a miracle just waiting to happen' and one that changed his life, and hers. If angels do exist, he states, then she was one of them, and how lucky was I to have met her!